D0821184

Close Your Eyes
When Praying

Close Your Eyes
When Praying

Virginia Cary Hudson

EDITED BY
CHARLES L. WALLIS

ILLUSTRATED BY
Susan Perl

1817

HARPER & ROW, PUBLISHERS

NEW YORK, EVANSTON, AND LONDON

Contents

TO MOTHER

Benedicite, omnia opera Domini
O ye Children of Men, bless ye the Lord;
praise him, and magnify him for ever.

—THE BOOK OF COMMON PRAYER

Mother loved the Bible, people, and words. To her very considerable knowledge of the Bible, she contributed a remarkably winsome capacity for retelling the great Bible stories in terms of the daily life she knew in Kentucky and the larger world through which she roved as occasion might permit.

For Mother the Bible was not so much a record of how God revealed Himself long ago to our fathers as it is a guide to the way God reveals Himself to their children. She spoke as naturally and as casually about Biblical personalities as she would about her neighbors and acquaintances. She was on speaking terms with many of them.

When someone might interrupt Mother during one of her expository talks and say, "But that's not in the Bible," Mother would smilingly reply, "It's in my Bible. You go back to your Bible, and see if you don't find it there." She meant that a Bible reader should read not only the lines but also between the lines.

Mother's affection for all kinds of people was reflected in the fascination with which she clung to the stories of Biblical personalities. Her Bible was a book of people, and she was forever detecting something worthwhile in the Biblical rogues and some blemishment in the Biblical heroes. For Mother, the church—to which she gave her time and labor without reservation—was not a place where she met her kind of people, but rather a congregation of

God's kind of people, meaning people of all sizes, shapes, dispositions, and needs. If the Lord is no respecter of persons, Mother felt she could not be.

Mother was blessed with a knack for storytelling. Her memory was a choir of echoes. She entranced people with her prancing recollections and her contagious humor. She was especially delighted to recall her own follies and foibles.

Mother was determined that "someday" she would write a book. She talked of this continuously, but for her that "someday" never came. Yet she did a great deal of writing, using whatever scraps of paper might be available when "inspired" moments came or when she had agreed to give a talk at a church or mission.

Mother was certain that her mind best worked when she had a pen in her hand. She almost never taught or spoke in public without a manuscript.

The congenial combination of Mother's love of the Bible, people, and words is found in *Close Your Eyes When Praying*, which contains a number of lessons for the women in her Sunday School class. There must surely have been many more such lessons, but perhaps Mother did not consider the others worth keeping.

The identities of particular persons and situations have been changed in this book. This is as Mother would have wished it, for she never knowingly did or said anything that might have caused another person to feel uncomfortable.

VIRGINIA CLEVELAND MAYNE

The Lord Calls Virginia To Teach the Deborahites and She Recalls Other Persons and Places

GOOD MORNING, SISTERS.

Last night at the precise moment when the hands on my old kitchen clock had achieved perpendicular perfection the phone rang.

Martha-Jane, a four-week veteran in my kitchen, answered without my saying so and without wiping from her hands the potatoes and butter she had been joining in the bonds of gastronomic wedlock.

"Yes'm, this is Miss Virginny's place."

Then with a hand flourish befitting a queen conferring knighthood upon a button-humble subject, Martha-Jane turned to me and said, "For you."

It was the Rector.

I could sense by the plaintive passion in his voice that he stood on the verge of the Red Sea awaiting the miracle of passage over dry land.

"Virginia," he said, "as you no doubt know, Sister Joanna was called Home this week. Tomorrow the Deborah Class will need a new teacher. While meditating upon this matter, the Lord spoke your name in my ear."

"Can you be sure, Rector, that it was my name?" I mumbled.

"I am certain."

"Can you be sure, Rector, that it was the voice of the Lord you heard?"

"As certain as though it came from the Burning Bush."

He asked if he might come by for a "few moments" to unburden his concern. I allowed that one of my roomers had only today achieved the distinction of thirty-one years, and at this very minute we were to have a little dinner party—fatted calf and all—in her honor.

"Then you will teach the Deborahites?" he ventured.

I have never knowingly turned from the voice of the Lord, but I hesitated momentarily.

"Well, as you may know, Rector, I have been a Rachelite for more years than I'd be likely to admit to. And I hanker for nothing more than to spend my declining years as a Rebekahite or perhaps a Lydiaite."

"But you will do this—for the Lord?" he persisted.

Just then I could smell the fatted calf burning in the oven.

So I said yes.

And here I am, a woman old enough to be the grandmother of your children, cast in the role of a lion thrown into a den of Daniels.

I cannot promise you much, but I'll give you all I've

got—a little common sense I've gleaned from tasting both bitter and sweet fruit and whatever wit and wisdom a merciful Lord has seen fit to share with me.

My credentials are these.

First, I have been a member in fairly good standing of this parish while four rectors have come and gone.

Second, I have done chore work for the Episcopalians among women in churches throughout Kentucky.

Third, although I have forgotten most the lessons in my Bible class in college—if I ever learned them—I read my Bible every day, Sundays excepted.

Fourth, I tithe all that the Lord in His gracious prodigality provides me.

Fifth, I am a sinner who has not, I trust, been forgotten by the Lord.

After today we will have lessons which center in some of the women in the Bible, meandering through the gallery wherein hang the portraits of both saints and sinners.

But today, having received no instantaneous illumination from beyond this world and having had little time to prepare, I shall mention some things about myself. Just enough to put you on your guard.

I have before me words which I wrote late last night and early this morning. Too much fatted calf brought too little sleep! I am not comfortable without a manuscript in my hands, but I shall always try to read as though I am not reading.

I am not as confident as are some of the brethren of the cloth who, when they open their mouths, know that the Lord will put words on their tongues. If the Lord ever has words for me to speak, He puts them in my pen.

Almost exactly thirty years ago, I spent the summer at my father's country house situated on a high cliff overlooking eighteen miles of the Ohio River.

11

Three months without plans and schedules can be wearisomely long.

One day in the county paper I read an article bemoaning the fact that too many children had failed in their school examinations. Feeling that the curriculum of a country school could not immerse me in water that was too deep, I went to the principal and offered my services as a tutor for any pupil of any grade in any subject. Free of charge.

Almost at once they began to come—the indolent, the discouraged, the indifferent, the defiant, and the dumb.

I attempted to inject into these children, along with their lessons and in ways coincidental to the same, the only thing that would suffice them after their books were read and closed and when their lives were over and done—namely, a lively and applicable faith in God.

These children carried wood, milked cows, hoed gardens, made beds, and ironed clothes. I wondered if I might sew a little contentment into the fabric of their lives. I told them that the most humble task, if it benefits and includes others, has in it an element of Christ.

I told them that at each end of the railroad tracks, which they saw every day, there was a large city: St. Louis and Louisville. In these cities were large houses filled with unfortunate children. No one had loved or cared for these children, and having little to do, they had gotten into serious and lifelong trouble. These houses have long rows of beds, and in these beds are blind and crippled children who will never have an opportunity to weed a garden and will never be able to use strong arms and legs to carry wood.

I also told them that there were other big houses called orphanages for children who do not have mothers and fathers. The children can remain in the orphanages for only a certain length of time. Then they have to go out into a very big world and make-do all by themselves. Some of the children don't even know where they have come from or who they are. For as long as they live, some of them will never know their real names.

So I told my pupils to thank God every day for their homes and their parents and for the opportunity and privilege to grow naturally, as Jesus grew, without the frustration of sorrow or the confusing foolishness of pretense.

I had hoped to have a Sunday Bible class for these and other children at the house, but I certainly did not anticipate a class of adults in the church.

There being no Episcopal church, I attended the Methodist church, persuading myself that God's Chosen People and John Wesley's offspring were kissing cousins. Before I knew it, thirty-five to fifty hard-working and earnest souls of simple corn-husking and hog-calling faith were seated on benches in front of me each Sunday morning.

Every Sunday eight or ten men strayed over from the men's Bible class at the Baptist church. I found a little not-too-pious satisfaction in this sheep stealing!

These country people had calloused hands and weather-beaten faces. They loved the Lord with all of their hearts and all of their considerable strength and all of their souls. One could not say that they did not love the Lord with all of their minds, but this was less noticeable. Yet they were trusting persons in whom innate wisdom represented a substantial substitute for acquired knowledge. Anyone who might think that he could pass off on them any high-toned theological flapdoodle which did not encompass sound reasoning would find himself entangled with a primitive God-given instinct that transcends all verbal debate.

In time this group included people from all available denominations except Catholicism. Some of them walked a distance of more than four miles.

Among them were two Jews, one a proprietor of a secondhand store and the other a most stylish-dressed owner of a general store.

Deprived by distance of their synagogue, these Jews were enthusiastically welcomed. If one day we are to sit with Abraham, Isaac, and Jacob in the Kingdom of Heaven, we'd do well to get into practice now!

In the study of the Old Testament we fifty or so Christians learned a great deal from these two Jews. I came to understand that if you study the history of the Jewish people without the assistance of Jews, you never really know it.

And I soon discovered that these Jews were more familiar with the New Testament than many of our baptized church members.

They spoke of Jesus as the greatest of the prophets, the one sinless, perfected, and final personification of righteousness. "He is the Perfect Example all men should follow," one of them explained, "but when the Messiah comes a second time for you Christians, He will be coming for the first time for us."

Rumor soon had it along that short stretch of the Ohio River that I, an Episcopalian, was attempting to get all of the class into the Methodist membership. Imagine! I laid the rumor to rest by saying with all of the fervency I could muster that I truly believed the Lord did not give a hoot where His people worshiped but greatly cared that they worshiped somewhere.

Then some of the brothers tried to corner me regarding baptism. I replied that Holy Baptism was an outward and visible sign of an inner grace—thank God for my patient and long-suffering catechist!—and that I was not terribly concerned whether the second birth was sealed in the waters of the Ohio River or with three drops of precious liquid drawn from the Jordan.

As I look back on the summer I suspect that the Methodist minister considered me to be a harmless annoyance. The local priest, on the other hand, volunteered his library for my use and offered to assist me in my research. My school Latin and the church Latin in his books presented a problem I was unable to master.

But I did find books I could read, and I drew from them what I could by way of teaching a little Biblical history. These people knew almost nothing about religious history, but they were hungry to learn and responded most attentively to everything I found in the books. History, they said, gave them a deep-rooted sense of sureness and strengthened the foundations of their faith.

All, that is, except one. Her halo was a stiffly starched sunbonnet, and she came to tell me that so-and-so said I was a-standing up in church a-telling the most outlandish old-time tales a body ever heard. Furthermore, I was a-playing like I could remember clean back to Moses and a-calling it history. Oughtn't nobody to pay no 'tention to no history, 'cause it ain't nothin' no ways.

I invited the Sister to come to the class, but she apparently lacked the derring-do.

That is the story of my first adventure as a Sunday School teacher. I was thirty years younger then, and the bird was on the wing.

When the summer was at an end, I gave the families and friends of this crazy quilt Bible class a picnic at the country house on that cliff above the Ohio River. Five sprawling acres of lawn was a fitting setting, and the Lord sent us a fine day. We had burgoo, made outdoors of course, and

15

served in tin cups. The hotter the day, they used to say in those parts, the better the flavor. And we had peppermint stick candy, peanuts, chewing gum, chewing tobacco (Baptists excluded), ice cream cones, soda pop, and, I was told, some home brew anonymously donated.

The picnic commenced with a chain prayer in which all of the preachers stood together holding hands. The chain prayer was my idea, and I sashayed the participants in such a way that two of the reverend brothers, who prepared to assault the devil each Lord's Day by demolishing each other's theology, should be joined in hands of prayer!

I soon began to wonder if the chain had a final link. The prayers brought forth a few lusty hallelujahs and many amens. Not "ahmens," but "a-mens." When the preachers were at last exhausted, there was hymn-singing assisted by expert clappers, who added zest and tempo.

Warmed up by the singing, hometown talent, without noticeable encouragement, stepped forward. The village blacksmith cuddled a battered banjo and the local bricklayer handled with remarkable dexterity a twelve-inch harmonica for an earth-trembling rendition of "O Susanna." To this day I cannot figure how the bricklayer played so vigorously without disarranging his bushy mustachio.

These performers were each given a pair of socks and a necktie.

Then the spinster sister music teachers, who wore sleigh bells on their wrists, played such rip-roaring duets as "Goodbye, My Lover, Goodbye" and "Bill Bailey, Won't You Please Come Home," on the piano.

For their strenuous and deafening feat, they were presented what they had told me they most wanted—two large bottles of Lydia E. Pinkham's Vegetable Compound.

Two L. & N. chefs, who made the burgoo, sang befit-

tingly "The Gospel Train," and for this effort received dollar-store suitcases.

And I should mention Brother Hezekiah, stuffy, solemn, and proper, whose mien unmistakably was suited to his role of cemetery caretaker and undertaker. When he stepped forward and pampered momentarily his long black beard, which covered his chest like a pall, I expected to hear some lugubrious lines from "Evangeline." But no! he broke into the unexpected gaiety of "Toot, Toot, Tootsie, Goodbye"!

As a reward he was given a pair of pajamas. It was an open secret thereabouts that his wife forced him to wear her discarded nightgowns, ruffles and all. I was told by somebody's cousin or half-brother that Hezekiah had actually been sitting on a tombstone one hot summer night in one of those discarded gowns, ruffles and all.

The four preachers, their heads together, wailed in close harmony the words of "Please Don't Talk about Me When I'm Gone." The crowd hooted and shouted gleefully. (It had been noised about that two were on the verge of being transferred.)

Each was given a cotton umbrella.

After the two Jews offered a commendable imitation of Harry Lauder and Sarah Bernhardt, I gave them—believe it or not—red-letter Testaments.

The Bible class picnic ended in a square dance competition, the prize being a donated Poland China sow. The screeching fiddle of the telegraph operator furnished the music, and a mysterious retired sea captain, whom Robert Louis Stevenson must have surely encountered somewhere, did the calling. How he ever got that far inland I'll never know. Over one eye he wore a well-worn black patch. The only personal information he had ever divulged concerning

18

himself was that a beautiful woman on Bali had popped out his eyeball.

The winners by a country mile were a couple from the next county who called themselves "Frankie and Johnny." I had been asked if I had "saw" them. I hadn't, but when I did I "knowed" that never in all creation had I "saw" anything quite like them.

"Johnny," tall, gaunt, and having shifty sea-green eyes, locomoted with the undulating movement of the double-jointed. His pants were so tight across his hips that the buttons bulged. Never in my life did I pray so fervently that thread would hold. All I remember about "Frankie" were her brick-red hair, toothpick legs, and gold front teeth.

Coming by private car from Louisville to attend this gala homespun gathering were eight of my father's cronies, all frequent visitors at the cliff house. These sophisticated city experts in matters judicial, financial, medical, and industrial so laughed at the antics of my hillbilly Bible class that their eyes were wet.

When they had left, I found on my dressing table a paper bag containing four hundred dollars and a note which read, "A little kitty for the Lord." I felt sure the Lord would want His ordained servants to have the money. The priest said no, but the four Protestant preachers blessed the Lord for leading them into green pastures.

The Methodist preacher, no doubt thinking of the summer's wear and tear on his benches, accepted his hundred dollars, saying, "Bless you."

The Baptist grinned and grinned, rocking back and forth from off his heels and onto his toes.

The Presbyterian seemed a little embarrassed.

But the Holy Roller almost rolled for joy. He urged me

to kneel with him while he thanked God for the gentlemen from the city. Then he called upon the sun and the
moon, the sleeping wheat seeds, and the golden waving
corn to bear testimony of this his material manna from
Heaven. It was indeed a heart-warming spectacle to behold!

Had he at that moment begun blasting the Catholics
in his praying as he did on the Lord's Sabbath in his
preaching, I should have felt, in all justice, duty-bound to
tug at the tail of his hand-me-down cutaway and suggest
that he not let his Protestant clutch out too fast. Had it
not been for the priest, his manna would have been less
sweet by several dollars.

During the picnic a stranger drifted in from off the
highway to learn what all the commotion was about.
Heretofore such carrying on in the name of the Lord had
most likely been unknown in those parts. No doubt he
suspected the founding of some new cult.

Worming his way through the crowd to welcome him,
I overheard him shout, "Where is this Miss Virginia, and
what does she believe in?"

To which the postmaster, ever eager to be of service,
answered with equal loudness: "Thar she is, right over
thar. The fat one. I would say, brother, that she believes
mainly in everything and mostly in nothing."

What a verdict. And after having struggled so hard to
bring about a little interdenominational harmony.

I was supposed to be a teacher of these people. In
reality I became their pupil. I learned from their simple
and unassuming instruction many lessons found in no
other source. I learned that in every condition and circumstance in life some spiritual gain can be reaped. In
their eyes I had seen registered the devotion and gratitude
of their hearts.

Life confines some of us in tight and cruel harness which

cramps our desire and cuts into the flesh of our spirit. Day by day we plow a hard and seemingly endless row.

Many women—and perhaps some of you—would have made excellent wives and wonderful mothers had not duty required you to stay at home. The Vestal Virgins were not the only women to devote their lives to a flame of a glowing undertaking—a clean flame which burns without the choking smoke of resentment and leaving no ashes of regret.

The road of life is a one-way highway. We have no choice but to go forward, for we cannot turn back. None wishes to be reminded that our common mortal destination is the grave.

Along the way many attractive and distracting signs advocate differing trends of thought and behavior. There is so much to be seen if we do not wear the blindfold of prejudice. There is so much to be done if we do not become paralyzed by selfishness.

The Creator of time and space has fixed our mileage to just one day at a time. Surely we can be entrusted with decency and honor for just one day.

And there are signals along the road for our personal safety. The serene green light of the conscience, the color of fertility and growth, tells us what is right. The warning red glare of the devil tells us what is wrong. The colors are not deceptive. Their contrast is easily discernible. A small child knows their difference. No man born of woman is morally blind. If everyone heeds these lights, the world will never know destruction.

On this road which all of us travel we find many puzzling intersections. The only authoritative markers are the commandments of God. They point at last to Jesus Christ, who is Himself the way.

Now, my dears, I'm not sure that this is the kind of

lesson the Rector had in mind. Perhaps he would not approve. If you have any doubts, please don't tell.

Next Sunday we shall turn to the beginning of all things, the story of Eve. Remember to bring your Bibles.

Before we take up the class offering, let us join in prayer. I ask only one thing: close your eyes when praying.

Virginia Tells How It All Began with Eve and Laments for Eve's Daughters

TODAY, SISTERS, we turn to the story of a woman. Being a woman myself, it is natural that I should tell the story as I see it. This means from a woman's point of view.

This story concerns Eve, the mother of us all. I think we can understand her, but I very much doubt if any man ever could.

Eve was God's first problem. I'm not persuaded that the good Lord knew what to make of her or what could be done about her.

She was a puzzle and a bewilderment to Adam, even as the daughters of Eve have always baffled the sons of Adam.

I hoped that the Bible commentators might offer me some guidance as I have sought to explore Eve's personality and predicament. But, alas, my reading proved futile.

One Bible commentator writes, "At best, Eve is an enigma." Imagine! What, I wonder, does he think that Eve is at worst?

Another Bible commentator comments, "Eve: the first woman." Brilliant! Another, flailing, as I imagine, his spectacles in one hand, wrote with a flourish of the other hand these astringent words: "Eve: the first sinner. *Ergo*, the mother of the sinful human race."

Bible commentators are what's wrong with the world today. If the good Lord, who never dropped a stitch, had wanted commentaries about His holy words, He would surely have included them in the Bible.

So let's leave the bewhiskered Bible commentators in their stuffy towers! Instead of their bloodless exposés about Eve—may she rest in peace!—let us consider her as only women can. What I shall read here is according to my own instinctive feelings.

But first I have a couple of announcements.

On the board I noticed that our collection last Sunday was thirteen dollars and two cents.

Thank God for the poor widow among us who did not neglect to give her two mites.

Each person here last Sunday gave on average twenty-two cents into the Lord's treasury.

The offering of the Rachelites was forty-seven dollars and eighty-three cents. But, of course, they are well-heeled and well-upholstered matrons, and there are twice as many of them.

The Good Book says, "Freely ye have received, freely give." That may explain the twenty-two cents. If your hard-working and provident spouses provide you two dollars and twenty cents a week, then, of course, you have done all that the Law and the Prophets require.

I might add parenthetically that, in all these years of hanging up Dad's pants, it didn't take me long to realize that loose change doesn't hang well. So I have always rescued it, lest it roll indiscriminately into some outlandish place like under the highboy. Just a hint.

Last Sunday I accosted Brother Gregory, the Caruso of the Gospel singers, and pleaded with him to bridle somewhat his insistence that all favorite hymns be sung during the opening exercises. I told him I needed each of the thirty little minutes which the Lord provides for the class lessons.

He said he sometimes got carried away on the wings of the Spirit but that he would search his heart for some message or direction on the matter.

Now we return to Eve.

If you find the lesson a bit raw, remember that we are dealing with Eve whom we find in the raw and that we are going to the very root of life which is a matter not to be minced.

Human eyes were not privileged to witness the greatest spectacle of all time—the creation of the universe.

Its majestic splendor can only be faintly imagined.

This never-completely-to-be-fathomed creation was surely the culmination of the Master Plan of the one and only creator, God.

The only thing that will ever match the dramatic creation of the universe will be its destruction. No man saw its creation. All men will see its ending.

Please turn now in your Bibles to the Book of Genesis, Chapter One, Verse One. Even if you don't read your Bible regularly, you shouldn't have too much trouble locating this particular reference!

In the beginning God.

These are the first four words of the Holy Bible. How or when that beginning was and from whence God evolved is, as my mother used to say, absolutely none of our business. Otherwise He would have told us.

In all baffling secrets which men so laboriously attempt to solve, they are forever halted with the one and only conclusion which spells G-O-D.

Some men say that they do not believe in God. Yet when they come to that last fundamental principle of all their searching, they can substitute no other word.

In the forms of all life, God has seen fit to separate these forms into different species or breeds. A Poland China is easily discernible from a razorback. A dray horse cannot compete with a thoroughbred. Nobody in his right mind mistakes an alley cat for a Persian. No sane man expects the throat of a sparrow to produce the song of a nightingale.

Do you follow me? All right then.

A hoodlum might pick your pocket, but never an aristocrat, to whom the word "theft" is most revolting. Of course, under jurisdiction of court the aristocrat might take the shirt off your back. Yet he would never, under any conditions, prove guilty of rudeness to you according to any accepted code of ethics.

A drunken bum might ravish a lady, but a gentleman, even if he had, shall we say, imbibed too freely, would never force his unwelcome attentions or intentions upon a member of the opposite sex. Now he might have an address book filled with the names of clandestine friends, but he would never conduct himself in a disorderly manner nor make himself obnoxious by inelegant remarks.

All of this is told us in the Good Book—somewhere. Perhaps not in so many words, however.

Our parentage is determined solely by the accident of our birth, and our nature is proven by the heritage we acquire in that parentage.

You no doubt have heard the Rector say as much many times.

26

These differences are dealt with accordingly by intelligent and discerning people, and the knowledge of them is most helpful in fitting together the jigsaw puzzle which we call life.

So much for the first four words in God's Word. Now turn to the next two verses.

And the earth was without form, and void. . . . And God said, Let there be light.

Our earth, our lives, and our purposes are void and without form if we do not let the revealing light of God shine upon them. Only the light of God sheds a true perspective on what is before us, and without His light we are in total spiritual darkness.

Now pass over the next several verses until you come to Verse Twenty-six.

And God said, Let us make man.

Who is "us"? Us was, is, and forevermore will be the triple Deity, one godhead of three separate persons—Father, Son, and Holy Ghost, God the Creator, His Son the Redeemer, and the directing Comforter. All work in unison toward the blending and perfecting of one ultimate and divine plan.

Now pass on to Chapter Two, Verse Eighteen.

And the Lord God said, It is not good that the man should be alone.

The saddest, the most empty, and the most futile of all lives are lived by those who deliberately shun association with other people.

From Adam's rib God fashioned Eve.

From Adam's side, that she might walk beside him and share his life. From beneath his arm, that he might always protect her. From under his heart, that he might ever cherish and love her.

That is how God intended it to be, although none of

the Bible commentators make even the slightest allusion to this fact.

Now, mind you, in the dawn of this new earth Eve suffered the unspeakable tragedy of having been created adult. When she gained consciousness, she found herself to be mature and placed in strange and startling surroundings to which she had not been permitted through the process of maturing to become gradually accustomed. She was without all of the contacts which normally make us what we are—parents, teachers, and friends, as well as prior example and influence. As such she was presented to Adam to be his helpmeet.

"Helpmeet" is one of those precious and gloriously archaic words in the Authorized Version which disturbs only those readers who have lost from their souls all poetic sentiment. It means "helper."

So Eve is given bodily, without preference or choice, to a man whom she had never before seen—to a complete stranger.

In the Bible passage under consideration there is the pathetic omission to any reference whatsoever to their personal feelings concerning each other or their relationship. Those of us who are romantically inclined would like to read here that Adam loved Eve. There is, however, not even the inference that Adam was even pleased with her or that he looked favorably upon her. In other words, Adam presumably said, "Get going, my little helpmeet, and see what you can do to make yourself useful."

A man could read these verses without any qualms, but not a woman. It breaks our hearts—as it must surely have broken Eve's sensitive heart.

Now trace back in your Bible to Verse Fifteen.

And the Lord God took the man, and put him into the garden of Eden to dress it and to keep it.

Even in this earthly Paradise, God from the very beginning expected Adam to assume responsibility. God did not want Adam to remain unoccupied. God expects every one of us to bestir ourselves and do that which will not only benefit ourselves but also glorify Him. We live in a garden that is just as much of God's own planting as that wherein Adam and Eve dwelt. In everything that we observe about us there is manifestation of God and opportunity for us to serve Him.

Back further now to Verse Nine.

The tree of life also in the midst of the garden, and the tree of knowledge of good and evil.

This tree even now is in our midst. From its roots flows the sap of spiritual survival. The tree stands vertically, suggesting the upward thrust of man's God-reaching desires, and is braced by God to withstand all storms that life brings to us.

Chapter Three.

Now the serpent was more subtil than any beast of the field which the Lord God had made.

Notice the word "subtil." In the field of life the things which shatter our hopes and break our hearts come within the category of subtility. Even death, which strikes with such sweeping force, has dignity and serves to establish our kinship with God. But the subtil things—malice, hatred, envy, greed, jealously, prejudice, slander, misrepresentation, distortion of the truth, injustice, and the manufacturing of lies—these things, fixing their beady and lidless and hence never-closing eye upon us, wind themselves about us and with a sting of venom poison our entire lives.

The snake of Eden was surely not so large as the snake usually depicted in Biblical art. Rather is it a horned cerastes, a very small snake, but as deadly as sin itself, and suggestive of how that which is wrong so often presents itself to us in small and seemingly harmless guise.

Now to Verse Four.

And the serpent said unto the woman.

I am not sure in what language the snake spoke to Eve. Snake-talk, no doubt. At any rate, Eve understood the syntax of the snake. And as a consequence poor Eve has been the clay pigeon toward which all of the pigeon-hearted theologians and estimable Bible commentators have taken aim with their popguns. As a result countless generations of otherwise relatively sane human beings have been bamboozled into believing that the daughters of Eve are the root of all evil.

But let us make no hasty judgment of our common mother. In all fairness we must admit that Eve did not know right from wrong, not yet having tasted of the fruit which was destined to reveal that knowledge. Therefore, I ask you, how could she be expected to deal wisely in the face of temptation, when her poor soul was entirely ignorant of both good and evil?

It is, of course, true that God had said of this particular fruit, "Thou shalt not eat of it." But disobedience is an equation of wrong, of which this innocent woman knew nothing.

She did, however, know that the fruit "was pleasant to the eyes." Every woman since time began has been enticed, enraptured, and enthralled by any and all things which are beautiful to look upon.

If we might take a little detour for a moment, I should like, once and for all time, to scotch the prevailing notion that this particular fruit was an *apple*. If you can find the word "apple" mentioned anywhere in the entire Book of Genesis, I will give you a good tip on the Derby! So not only Eve but also the apple has been maligned by those Bible readers who are forever reading their own prejudices and preferences into God's Holy Word. Tell me, furthermore, where in the Bible we are told that Jonah was swal-

lowed by a *whale* or that the number of wise men who worshiped at the manger of our Lord was *three?*

When Eve discovered that the fruit was beautiful to look upon, what did she do? Sit down before it, hoping for ample time—an eon or two perhaps—to contemplate its beauty? Oh, no! The very first thing that came into her mind was that this beautiful fruit was also good for food—something she might give to her husband.

I dare say that since time began every man has been waiting for his little helpmeet to bring him something good to eat. I can just picture Adam stretching himself in the long, green grass, smacking his lips, and sniffing the air in anticipation of what Eve might bring him to eat.

And can't you see poor Eve climbing trees and shaking their branches, scratched from harvesting a berry patch, digging and scraping in the field in order that she might cope with Adam's hunger?

The Fall was a consequence not of Eve's curiosity but of Adam's appetite.

Apart from his cowardly blaming of Eve in order to save his own skin, there are only two important things said in the Bible concerning Adam. These are that "he ate" and "he begat." How many of his descendants to this very day seem chiefly to be interested in only these two pastimes!

Now turn to Verse Eight.

The Lord God walking in the garden in the cool of the day.

That seems to me to be a most fitting time for the Lord to have walked in His garden. The stillness that encompasses the world at that particular hour is an expectant hush awaiting the voice of God. God always seems nearer to us when day is done. Small wonder that nightfall has ever been man's favorite time to commune with God in prayer.

32

And what did the Maker of heaven and earth say to His frightened children?

Where art thou?

What is this that thou hast done?

Sooner or later each person who lives will hear the voice of God call to him or her and ask these same age-old questions. When day is done or when life is done, God will speak, and we shall stand before God naked and ashamed.

The spiritual wardrobes even of the saints seem hardly adequate. We have been stripped of honesty by ambition, stripped of truth by lying words and deeds, and stripped of all kindness by meanness. Adam and Eve are at the head of a long list of those who stand before the Lord wearing nothing except shame only.

In Verse Twelve are found the shortest crutches on which any man has ever limped.

The woman whom thou gavest to be with me, she gave me of the tree, and I did eat.

In Eve's darkest hour, Adam let her down. Having utterly no sense of loyalty, no sense of protection, and no sense of pity, he blamed her for his own weakness. An alibi as old as the world! Cringing and whining before God, Adam did not care what might become of Eve. As far as he was concerned, she was on her own.

By succumbing to a half-truth, Adam hoped to prove himself blameless. But Eve was not a coward. Openly and frankly she told God the only thing there was to tell. What was this? That the serpent had told her to eat.

In all of this there was something too big for Eve's understanding. She expected some kind of explanation, but she received none. Standing all atrembling before the Almighty, she awaited an answer.

What did God say?

I will greatly multiply thy sorrow.

And tears filled the eyes of Eve.

I do not question but that the judgments of God are altogether righteous. Yet when I read the solemn words which stencil out the curse upon Eve, I cannot help thinking of the loving father whose anxious eyes searched the distant horizon for the returning Prodigal whom he would embrace in love and to whom he would give the boon of a second chance. Or of Christ's inspiring injunction that we should forgive another man not once but seventy times seven times.

Eve was told that in sorrow she should bring forth her young.

And so it was.

And so it ever has been.

The anxiety that attends birth continues for a mother to the end of her life. Concern for your child's mental and physical growth. Concern for its permanent well-being. Concern for the salvation of its soul. Concern for those with whom it associates. Concern with failures and achievements.

Perhaps the greatest of all sorrows is that of being unable to exchange places with our children when the crushing experiences of life seem almost to overwhelm them.

God told Adam and Eve, "Be fruitful, and multiply, and replenish the earth."

The woman whom God placed on this earth for that express purpose bore three children, Cain, Abel, and later, after one son had been slain, Seth. I have heard tell that God thereby considers two children to be a sufficient quota.

Because Abel seemed to have been more favorably regarded by the Lord than himself, Cain slew his brother. Jealousy transforms men into monsters. I think Cain, who had no true concept of the nature and finality of death, surely did not premeditate anything so disastrous.

But imagine Eve's horror when she looked upon her dead lad. How she must have held his cold body against her own in a vain effort to warm it. How she must have called to him again and again, hoping that he might speak to her.

Between the lines of Holy Scripture I would like to add these words: "And when he that was first dead upon the earth was covered by the earth, the mother of all living cried unto God, saying, 'Oh, give me back my boy.' But neither God nor her reason answered her, and looking about she girded herself to live."

The most pure, holy, unchanging, unselfish, and God-given love on earth is the love of a mother for her child. The tears Eve shed over the body of Abel never ceased.

But, looking about, Eve saw the need of her husband and her surviving son for her, and "she girded herself to live." She steeled herself for her battle with grief and with life's continuing responsibilities.

You Deborahites are soon-to-be-marrieds, recently-marrieds, and not-long-since marrieds. I beg you to remember Eve. For many a mother, like Eve, life is a long battle without furlough or medal. All soldiers do not wear uniforms, and many who are brave receive no decorations.

Eve's sorrow was compounded when the Lord drove Cain away from his kith and kin. God's judgment on Cain fell with an equal or greater weight upon Eve. Abel dead and Cain exiled.

The cursed Cain, Eve felt, would need her now more than ever. How her heart went after him. Never again would she know where he was or how he fared.

Nod, the land into which Cain was driven, was east of

Eden. It was toward the east that Eve looked anxiously day after long day. It is toward the east that we look for the rising of the sun and the promise of a new day, a new beginning, a new chance. It is toward the east that all faithful men look for the coming again of the Son of Righteousness.

And Adam knew his wife again; and she bare a son, and called his name Seth.

God did not send Seth to take the place of Abel. Every mother knows that one child cannot replace another. A true mother never loves one child more than another. Our children come to represent different things to us, each filling a distinct place which is irreplaceable by another. One child is more affectionate, one more generous, one more understanding, one more dependable. One child swells our pride; another stirs our pity.

Yet Eve must surely have been comforted by the birth of Seth. And now she could experience what every mother covets, an opportunity to inspire and guide a child in ways she may previously have attempted without altogether satisfying success.

The story of Eve is in a way the story of the earth's most pathetic woman, cursed and punished for something she never fully understood, placed alone in a garden with a man who was a stranger to her, forced to make-do without a mother's patient instruction, and the devil always seeking to make her stumble.

Personally I think she did remarkably well in a rather hopeless circumstance, just as many women are still doing today.

My dears, my meanderings through the story of Creation have come to an end. I am at the bottom of the twenty-eighth page of my notebook which, according to my calculations, is all of the pitifully short time provided for the lesson each Lord's Day. But there are other Sundays and other Biblical women whose mystique we shall attempt to explore.

Now before we gather the tithes into the storehouse, let us join together in a closing prayer. Remember, please, to close your eyes when praying.

Virginia Explains How Rachel's Unloved Sister Leah Claims in Death What Life Denied Her

SISTERS IN THE LORD.

The membership committee, that is, Dorothy Martin, reports that this morning we have five guests. If it is their wish—and if they return after today—they will become members of our class, and then it will be our privilege of taking unto our bosom, as it were, five capable and understanding sisters.

Each of these women, while being entirely different from any one of us, is yet fundamentally like us.

Each one will come to mean a different thing to us, and the combination of the five of them will serve our common purpose.

To fully enjoy the privilege of our association with these women—and in order to draw the best from them for ourselves and to offer the best to them of ourselves—it is first necessary that we come to know them.

So will you please make yourselves known, exchange

names and addresses, and engage in that kind of small talk that always seems to anticipate or precipitate friendship.

But please, oh, please, don't extend your felicitations into the Rector's sermon hour!

Now where Sunday School is concerned, some people say they can take it or leave it. I will not quarrel with them. Yet let me say this one word. To those of us who are privileged to live in this awesome generation has been given the greatest challenge in the history of civilization.

The heart of the world is breaking, and there is no better channel in which women can row against this universal outrage than through the Church.

And so to our guests I say, your interest is our incentive, your presence is our encouragement, your membership represents your approval, and your attendance will be our reward.

Today I want to talk about two Bible women. They are the wives of Jacob, by name Rachel and Leah. Their story is told in Genesis, Chapter Twenty-nine and following.

After Jacob had roughened up his brother Esau by depriving him of both birthright and blessing, his ever-scheming mother Rebekah told him that he had better make tracks and quickly. His dull-witted brother was certain to seek revenge.

So Rebekah told Jacob to run for his life, and she told him where to run to—way off into Mesopotamia to Padan-aram, some five hundred miles away, and her old family home. There Jacob would have outdistanced his brother's wrath, and there he might just happen to find himself a wife from among his own kinsmen.

You know the story of Jacob and Rachel. Everyone does.

The weary-worn outcast came at last to his mother's home, where the first person his eyes fell upon was a slim and trim little shepherdess who just happened to be his own cousin and the most likely marriage prospect one might hope to find anywhere.

When Jacob looked upon this daughter of nature, his heart was immediately taken. How does Genesis describe this meeting? "And Jacob kissed Rachel, and lifted up his voice, and wept."

I presume Rachel wept also. No doubt she had wondered when and if ever a storybook knight might come on a camel and claim her lovely little hand.

Meanwhile her father Laban, sensing the inevitable, said yes before Jacob asked. But he suggested a condition or two. To wit, that Jacob should do a little work about the place for a little time, and then he could have Rachel scot-free.

Everyone seemed pleased. Jacob would get a comely wife. Rachel would have time to fill her hopechest. And Laban would get some cheap labor.

So "Jacob served seven years for Rachel; and they seemed unto him but a few days, for the love he had to her."

Which is about the nicest compliment ever paid to any woman anywhere in world literature.

And since then writers, poets, and artists have been trying to outdo the writer of Genesis in attempting to improve upon the grace and beauty of Rachel.

At the end of seven years, Jacob went to Uncle Laban to ask for what was coming to him.

But Laban, who was as much of a schemer as his sister Rebekah, had other plans. The Bible tells what he did better than I can, so I will let the Bible speak for itself.

> And Laban gathered together all the men of the place, and made a feast.
> And it came to pass in the evening, that he took

Leah his daughter, and brought her to him; and he went in unto her. . . .

And it came to pass, that in the morning, behold, it was Leah: and he said to Laban, What is this thou hast done unto me? did not I serve with thee for Rachel? wherefore then hast thou beguiled me?

And Laban said, It must not be so done in our country, to give the younger before the firstborn.

Well, who is this Leah whose face Jacob saw in the morning light? She was Rachel's older sister. But no one in his right mind would serve seven years for Leah. Why? "Leah was tender eyed; but Rachel was beautiful and well favoured."

Need I say more?

To speak bluntly, Leah was dull-eyed, which is a euphemism for saying that she was homely. No doubt her red eyes were a consequence of her crying because her little sister had got all the good looks.

Leah had long been a problem and a concern for Father Laban. What to do? No man was likely to want her, and how long could he be expected to provide her berth and board? If she couldn't get a husband for herself, then he would have to take a hand.

So Jacob became the fall guy. Besides, if he really wanted Rachel, he could also have her in exchange for another seven years of servitude.

Thus Jacob got two wives. The one he loved passionately, and the other he hated just as passionately. And she knew it.

The Bible commentators pass off Leah with a few patronizing words. That is the way of the world. "Too bad about Laban's elder daughter. She's a nice enough girl, but— She ought to be happy to get a husband by hook or crook."

But Leah wasn't happy. How must she have felt when her father, thinking so little of her sensitivities, made her an unwilling partner in his scheme to defraud the man her sister loved? How must she have thought when the man her father deceived looked for the first time behind her veil and despised her? How does any woman feel to know that her husband does not love her? Jacob put up with Leah and he tolerated her presence, but nowhere in the Bible do we read that Jacob loved Leah—ever.

One summer night years ago a loose-jointed son of a former family servant knocked at our kitchen door. He twisted his gray cap in his grimy hands. His mouth hung open in despair.

"Miss Virginny," he said, "Pappy needs you."

In a moment he disappeared, but his words conveyed a world of meaning to me.

I found Pappy in the hospital. His features were ashen, and his throat rattled as he spoke. The city doctors had carved on old Pappy, and he could not linger much longer in this world.

"I'm about run out of time," he said, "and the devil is already rampanting after my soul. But I want you to pray for me, Miss Virginia, honey. Talk pretty to my Jesus for me, please, Ma'am. Ask Him to let me die peaceful like, and just kind of glide away to Glory."

I knelt at the bed, and words from the Prayer Book took audible form.

"O Father of mercies, and God of all comfort, our only help in time of need: we fly unto thee for succour in behalf of this thy servant, here lying in great weakness of body . . ."

"That sure sounds pretty," he whispered.

I continued. ". . . unfeigned repentance . . . stedfast

faith. . . . rest with all thy saints in the eternal habitations. . . . thy dwelling-place in the Paradise of God. . . ."

Before the last amen, Pappy interrupted "One thing more, Miss Virginia. Just one thing more. Tell the good Lord for me, please, Ma'am, that if Lulu Belle gets to strutting on my insurance money, I hope He haunts her forevermore."

It is my firmest conviction that the Lord provides for His children by giving each one the wherewithal to live a good and worthy life. Leah might not have been possessed of Rachel's beauty and she might not have been as well-favored, but God provides an asset for each deficiency.

Someone has said that compensation means that if your left arm is shorter than your right arm, then your right arm is longer than your left arm.

I guess that is right.

Someone has also said that God never closes one door without opening another.

I know that is right.

If Rachel's outward features were satisfying to the eye, Leah's inner life brought her a measure of satisfaction through service.

Jacob may have hated Leah, but he was not above claiming sons from her hands. While Rachel languished in barrenness, Leah produced six sons and one daughter. "And when Rachel saw that she bare Jacob no children, Rachel envied her sister; and said unto Jacob, Give me children, or else I die." Her plea was answered only after Leah's children were well on their way toward maturity. Then Rachel gave birth to Joseph and later to Benjamin, although ironically and tragically Benjamin's birth required her own life.

Yet to the end of Rachel's life she had Jacob's love. This Leah was denied.

44

There is a heart-rending pathos attending the birth of Leah's sons.

When Reuben, the first-born, came, Leah herself selected his name, "for she said, Surely the Lord hath looked upon my affliction; now therefore my husband will love me."

But he did not.

When Simeon, the second-born, came, Leah so named him "because the Lord hath heard that I was hated" and "hath therefore given me this son also."

But Jacob's heart was a stone.

When Levi came, Leah said, "Now this time will my husband be joined unto me, because I have born him three sons."

Still Jacob so loved Rachel that he had no love for Leah.

When Judah came, Leah said, "Now will I praise the Lord."

The voice of Jacob did not join in these praises.

When Issachar came, Leah said, "God hath given me my hire," and when Zebulun came, Leah said, "God hath endued me with a good dowry; now will my husband dwell with me, because I have born him six sons."

But Jacob's heart was too small to include any except Rachel.

Deprived of her husband's love, Leah gave herself wholeheartedly to her children.

She taught them the fear of the Lord. Leah was devoted to Jacob's God, who is our God. When Rachel stole her father's idols—the story is recorded in Genesis Thirty-one —she apparently still trusted in pagan deities. But not so with Leah.

Leah loved her children through childhood and into maturity. And with what results?

Reuben stayed the hands of his understandably agitated brothers when they wished to put to death their arrogant and shamefully boastful and spoiled half-brother Joseph, and he was the father of the first of the twelve tribes of Israel.

The sons of Levi were for countless generations charged with the interpretation and keeping of the Law and represented the priesthood in Israel.

Judah was the ancestor of Boaz, Jesse, David, Solomon, and, according to St. Luke, of our Lord.

Perhaps Leah knew in her heart of hearts that many would arise who might find blessing because of the love she bore her children. I hope so.

But this is not the end of Leah's story.

When Rachel died in childbirth, Jacob buried her in Bethlehem. Jacob, now an older and wiser man, found some measure of strength in the strength of Leah. Not having Rachel by his side, he may have discerned, though retardedly, that Leah possessed rare qualities, if not of the face, at least of the heart and head.

I think this is true.

After Rachel's death, Jacob "set a pillar upon her grave," but when Leah died, what did Jacob do? He took her mortal remains to Machpelah where they were deposited in a cave which Abraham had selected as the burial place for himself and his wife Sarah. There his parents, Isaac and Rebekah, were buried. And there, in due time, Jacob was also laid to rest.

I think that Jacob came at last to recognize those sterling qualities which Leah had possessed since childhood.

I think that Jacob deliberately chose to be placed in death by the side of one who had remained faithful and hopeful till death.

Strange, isn't it, that Rachel, the beloved, should finally

be laid to rest in wind-swept loneliness outside of Bethlehem and that Leah, the rejected, should slumber until Judgment Day with the patriarchs and next to him whose slightest attention had always thrilled her inexpressively.

I do not judge Jacob and Rachel. That is the prerogative of God only. But the role which Leah unwillingly was required to play in the drama of life is not unlike that of many another woman.

Were I to choose for my daughters between the beauty of outward feature of Rachel and the inward beauty of Leah, I should choose Leah's beauty, although I know my choice would bring pain and sorrow.

I think the long expanse of Old Testament history records no more pathetic story than that of Leah. The only parallel stories are those of Tamar, who was loved and hated by her stepbrother, or the daughter of Jephthah, whose foolish father bartered her life for military victory, or the unnamed mother of the wicked Canaanite chieftain Sisera who, awaiting the return of her warrior son, "looked out at a window, and cried through the lattice, Why is his chariot so long in coming? why tarry the wheels of his chariots."

I think God transformed Leah's loss into gain. And I am sure he will do the same for you, if you hold fast to the faith, as Leah did.

On such an uplifting note I will close the lesson. But first our prayer and then the class offering.

Virginia Bemoans the Lord's Day and Finds Something Good in Bathsheba

GOOD MORNING, SISTERS.

I am reminded this morning of the beautiful and venerated words by one of Israel's sweet-tongued poets: "This is the day which the Lord hath made; we will rejoice and be glad in it."

Do you remember the words of the old hymn?

> O day of rest and gladness,
> O day of joy and light,
> O balm of care and sadness,
> Most beautiful, most bright.

What matchless sentiments!

But don't believe them. The words were written by men.

What is the Lord's Day for womenfolk?

O day of noise and commotion—when the children are home from school!

O day of rushing and serving—when hubby, freed from the toils of the workaday world, lounges and loafs and clutters.

O day of cooking and dishwashing—when everyone wants fried chicken for dinner, ham for supper, and "something to fill us up" before bedtime.

O day of gobble and gobbledegook—when distant friends, long-lost relatives, and nonkissing cousins drop by "for just a moment"—providentially just at eating time—and leave long after the sidewalks have been rolled up for the night.

Who ever said that the day following was a "blue Monday"? Monday is in fact the "day of all the week the best."

The next thirty minutes represent a reprieve from all of this. At this time we can be women in our rights, talk like women, think like women, and glory in our womanliness.

Last Sunday the Rector said he had not seen many Deborahites at the eleven o'clock Morning Prayer and Service. I assured him that the Deborahites had no members who slipped out the side doors and that, if he wishes, we would parade behind our class banner into the sanctuary and down the center aisle.

Our lesson today is about Bathsheba.

If in hearing this story you detect what sounds like an element of disparagement, bear in mind that I am merely exposing the frailties of our common, fickle human nature. A story such as this one assures us that God loves us in spite of what we are and that He longs for us to realize what we may become if we open our minds and hearts to His infinite mercy and benediction.

Generally speaking, women are stamped with the indelible hallmark of their husbands' material standing. The house a woman lives in, the clothes she wears, and even the car she drives are dead giveaways, not of what he is, but of who he is and what he has. Even his death does not remove his stamp, for what he manages to leave her determines the manner in which she continues to subsist.

Hidden beneath the façade of material success, however, is often stamped unhappiness. Under the most costly garments there sometimes beats the heaviest heart.

All of this was true concerning Bathsheba.

Encircling this beautiful woman was the binding and inseparable chain of her husband. To understand the conditions under which she labored, it is necessary to consider him.

David, the eighth son of Jesse of Bethlehem, is described as "a comely person," "valiant," "a man of war," and "a cunning player on an harp"—a perfect combination of attributes becoming a ladies' man. His appeal to women permeates the written record of his entire life.

Women on two occasions saved his life.

A woman was sent by Joab to persuade him.

A woman wrung a decision from him at the behest of the prophet Nathan.

Women cheered and shouted when he danced joyously before the Ark, thereby kindling the fury of Saul.

A woman was responsible for the alienation between him and his son Absalom, whose beauty, the Bible says, was without blemish and had stolen the hearts of Israel away from David as easily as David had previously captivated them.

Abigail, the first woman whom David claimed, had encouraged him when she made a visit, of which "she told not her husband," to see him. When her husband Nabal learned of this, "his heart died within him, and he became as a stone." Hearing of Nabal's death, David exclaimed, "Blessed be the Lord." Thereupon David dispatched messengers, who approached Abigail, saying, "David sent us unto thee, to take thee to him to wife." What was the young widow's response? "And she arose, and bowed herself on her face to the earth, and said, Behold, let thine handmaid be a servant to wash the feet of the servants of my lord." That she came unto David accompanied by five damsels surely did not lessen David's enthusiasm.

Dear Sisters, do I exaggerate the story of Israel's greatest king, a towering tree on the horizon of world history, and a man, as the pious historian says, after God's own heart? Turn to the Book of First Samuel, and you will find everything I have said clearly documented.

And there was Michal, sister of David's bosom friend Jonathan and daughter of David's enemy Saul. King Saul felt that he might gain the upper hand if David were to become his son-in-law. Michal was a willing pawn, for, the Bible tells us, she "loved him." But she turned the tables on her father and by a clever feminine ruse—remember the feigned sickness and the idol she stuffed in the bed?—helped David to escape from the wrath of her father.

When Saul's continued enmity toward his son-in-law separated the young lovers, the king gave Michal in marriage to a man named Phaltiel.

Years later, after David had become King of Israel, succeeding Saul, he still coveted Michal. When Ishbosheth —that's a name for you!—took Michal away from her hapless husband, David cared not an iota for Ishbosheth's welfare. Phaltiel's devotion to Michal was no match for royal prerogative and power. As Michal was being carted off to David's harem, poor Phaltiel "went with her along weeping behind her" until he was driven back.

And then, of course, there was Bathsheba, the wife of Uriah the Hittite.

They say that the third time is the charm. This brazen and beauteous charmer flaunted her unadorned beauty at the garden pool at the very hour David was wont to stroll upon his rooftop. When David saw that she "was very beautiful to look upon," Uriah's goose was cooked.

David had in his army of Judah some five hundred thousand men and in the army of Israel eight hundred thousand men, or a total of one million three hundred thousand. Among this vast horde only thirty-seven are cited for might and valor. Among the thirty-seven is numbered Uriah the Hittite.

But David could hardly have been expected to have concerned himself in as trifling a matter as that of a marriage bond. So David had this particular husband summoned to the palace. David asked Uriah "how the people did, and how the war prospered." He poured a drink for Uriah. Then another and still another—until Uriah passed out and slept.

After this David told his sidekick Joab, "Set ye Uriah in the forefront of the hottest battle, and retire ye from him, that he may be smitten, and die."

Sure enough, an arrow of the adversary smote Uriah. After an appropriate period of mourning—state funeral, etc., no doubt—"David sent and fetched" Bathsheba and "she became his wife, and bare him a son."

Far be it from me to deprecate Israel's greatest king, but facts are facts.

I am not recalling this sordid story in an attempt to

outdo the Sunday newspaper supplement, but rather to express a truth that is bigger than David and all of us sinners combined.

God has an unfailing way of balancing His scales. Those who suffer injustice, He rewards. Those who offend His holy laws, He punishes. There is an inescapable clause in the economy of Heaven.

So God laid David low by the deaths of the only two persons David ever truly loved, Jonathan and Absalom.

When David sent for Mephibosheth, the son of Jonathan, to give him a home, Mephibosheth stood before him lame in both feet. Surely David must have felt that this was an ironic condemnation.

When at long last word was brought to David that his rebellious son Absalom was dead, the brokenhearted king lamented in words which surely must be the most poignant in the Old Testament: "O my son Absalom, my son, my son Absalom! would God I had died for thee, O Absalom, my son, my son!"

In the case of Bathsheba, the will of God came to David from the lips of the prophet Nathan. Bathsheba's child must die—and on the seventh day this was what happened.

Only those who, like myself, have placed our firstborn into a little casket and have turned our faces when the lid was lowered can fully sympathize with Bathsheba. We alone know the piteous and lifelong feeling which results from bearing a child and then surrendering it to the grave. As long as we live, we have an indescribable yearning to know what that child might have looked and been like and what it might have said and done. If a later child disappoints us or brings us sorrow, we always feel that had the first one lived, everything would have been so different.

The story of Bathsheba is the story of an adulteress who, seeking the forgiveness of God, found that His merciful arms embraced even her.

An old manuscript reads:

> And the child being dead, Bathsheba went daily into
> the temple to pray, saying, forgive me this mine own
> sin and stay thou now, O Lord, thine hand from me,
> and help me to find thy way.

Bathsheba may once have lacked sexual morality, but she
did not lack the spiritual courage to admit her sin and ask
for His guidance. Neither did she lack the moral stamina
to keep herself in God's way after she had been shown it.

She relinquished any ambition, had she ever had it, to
become Miss Israel of 1000 B.C. Instead, by the very
conduct of her life, she became honored and beloved.
Even the prophet of God turned to her in counsel. And
she earned David's utmost confidence and trust.

In David's last days, the high and the mighty and the
not-so-high came to him with news of all that was wrong,
saying, "Behold this" and "Behold that" and "Behold the
other." Realizing that he must soon join his fathers, David
knew that the time had come for him to give his final
orders to someone who could be trusted with them and to
someone having the brains and courage to carry them out.

It was then, when life was ebbing away, that David
said, "Call me Bathsheba."

Those three words tell us how much he revered her and
how much he depended on her. To her he gave directions
involving an entire nation, and it was she who completed
them.

Bathsheba lived to see her second son Solomon build
the temple of all temples ever to adorn the earth. On the
occasion of its dedication she heard the voice of her son
lifted in praise and thanksgiving, an audible and resound-
ing echo of the silent words within her own heart.

In His benediction of forgiveness, God both blessed
and sustained Bathsheba. I like to think that He purposely

waited until she was dead and gone before Solomon made such an all-fired fool of himself when he was old enough to know better.

You may wonder how Solomon, endowed with wisdom, could have behaved so foolishly. We do not always use all that God gives us. Many a man's talent has been buried by the soil of circumstance. Many a brainy man, capable of doing something astonishingly good, has been too slothful to bestir himself to useful action.

When it comes to the way of a man with women, Solomon was not the first, and surely not the last, to play the role of a fool. Leander, battling the waves of the Hellespont, seems insignificant in comparison to the deep water men allow themselves to be engulfed in because of a woman.

Our parish has not always been free from likely examples of all this.

But let us return to Bathsheba before Brother Gregory threatens our eardrums when he sounds the closing bell!

There was no smallness in Bathsheba's make-up.

She was without the jealous cruelty of Sarah, who so bedeviled her husband that he aided her in sending another woman into the wilderness to perish.

When Hagar presumed that nothing remained for her except death, she heard the voice of God. Many of us, like her, find God in the wilderness of bereavement, tragedy, and devastating disease.

God is in every wilderness, but if we moan and groan and screech and bawl, we shall never hear His voice. If we will only be still and listen, He will call out to us as surely as there is a Heaven and an earth.

Bathsheba was without the bickering of Rebecca, who was forever quarreling with her daughter-in-law and who was so unstable in her maternal maturity as to play favorites between her children and to become instrumental in persuading the child she favored to enact a lie before the blind eyes of his father.

Bathsheba was without the envy of Rachel, who hated her very own sister, and without the stealth she showed when through beguiling deception she stole her father's household gods.

And Bathsheba was without the deceitfulness of the great Queen Esther, who not only hid her own identity from her husband, but also, adorning herself in baubles and finery, stuffed his stomach with fine food and drink and then inveigled him into hanging his closest friend and confidant.

These virtuous patriarchesses employed at times such devious schemes that had I to make a choice among them of one with whom to risk my life, my possessions, or my reputation, I should surely prefer Bathsheba whose only offense was that of being enamored by a dashingly handsome king.

Bathsheba was neither pompous, haughty, nor proud. After David's death she proved to be a fearless exponent and a stanch and diplomatic leader. King Solomon showed his unbounded confidence in her when he said that whatsoever she might ask she might have. Her selfishness is demonstrated in the fact that for herself she asked absolutely nothing. The only requests she ever made of David and Solomon were relative to others, never herself. As when she interceded in behalf of her husband's son by another woman when he was not man enough to do his own asking.

Bathsheba must surely have been as conscientious and untiring as a mother as she was dutiful and loyal as a queen. Solomon was never separated from his mother as were Moses, Samuel, Joseph, and our Lord. In childhood he was never isolated in a monastic atmosphere of rigid religious training. The crowning act of Solomon's entire life reflects, like a shining mirror, the teaching of childhood, which we know was that of his mother. Constant association with Bathsheba instilled in Solomon such an ardent desire to serve his Maker that, when told he might have anything he wished, he showed humility of spirit and earnestness of purpose in choosing wisdom.

Bathsheba's beauty and dignity of person were sufficient to grace any occasion. Even in her waning years, she must have made Solomon's many wives seem pale by comparison, for Solomon extended to her his hand and asked that she should sit next to the throne.

Beloved of her husband, beloved of her son, and beloved of a people—such a reward was well-earned and justly deserved.

The story of Bathsheba is a lasting memorial to God's saving grace of those who come to Him in humble and sincere penitence and who seek His way and continue in the same.

None of this comes from the commentaries wherein Bathsheba is generally condemned out of hand. The astigmatic Bible reading of the bearded commentators does not permit them to see where the real and revealing truth lies. But I have found it, as you may find it, because the lesson is stenciled upon the heart of every wife and mother.

Dear friends, I thank you for being patient while an oldish woman talks. Store up this week sufficient patience to get you through my lesson next week.

Before collecting the collection and then awaiting the Lord's word as interpreted by the Rector, let us pray. And remember what your fuddy-duddy teacher asks: Close your eyes when praying.

Virginia Admits a Weakness and Contemplates Heaven

SISTER DEBORAHITES.

SISTER DEBORAHITES.

I must mention a matter of gravest urgency before we get into our lesson today.

My name and reputation have been shamefully blackened by persons unnamed because apparently last Lord's Day we dillydallied here beyond the "customary closing hour." I am being called "long-winded," and I plead guilty—a congenital weakness. I am being called a "wind-bag," and I plead the innocence of a newborn lamb!

Not too long ago we lived in a large apartment house where many remarkable things took place. It was our diverting pleasure to have as a near neighbor within these unusual walls one of Old King Cole's true brothers. He was verily a merry old soul. But it was only for his pipe and his most difficult grandson that he called. The latter did not have to be called often, for he was an inveterate hanger-on. So much so that the merry old soul had little time to listen to the strains, however sweet, from the fiddlers three.

On one particular night it fell to the lot of this generally merry grandsire to put his small grandson to bed.

This prolonged, rebellious, and exhausting task provoked the old man to wrath.

"Come here, you blasted rascal," stormed the grandfather to his small charge. "Get down there and pray. Do you hear me? Pray!"

Whereupon there wafted heavenward the petitions of a calm little voice:

God bless Grandmother,
God bless Grandfather,
God bless the Parkers,
God bless the Church,
God bless the Missions,
God bless the Heathens,
God bless the Grocery Man,
God bless the Milk Man . . .

On and on, fervently, earnestly, solemnly, he prayed.

His grandfather's erstwhile holy attitude was slowly replaced by anxious impatience.

"Hey there you!" he called, plucking the pious pleader by his night clothes. "Enough is enough! You'll exhaust both God and me. Now get up from there, and quit that praying. I want to fix myself a julep!"

I suppose when talking about the Lord I partake of the boy's weakness.

When I was born, my mother wanted a son who would grow up to be a preacher. What she got was a girl who grew up preaching.

I hope that I won't bore you if I say a little something about myself. It may help you to understand me a little.

Several years ago I was stricken with a dangerous and serious ailment. I was a poor surgical risk. I am not young. I am too fat. I have a faulty heart. More than one operation was indicated, because both kidneys were equally involved.

On the day I arrived at Johns Hopkins I was told that

two of the world's leading urologists were about to visit the hospital. One was the head surgeon at Mayo's and the other the outstanding man in his field in London. Between their lectures they would be told of my case, and I was assured that their advice would be sought. Each in turn offered his services—without charge.

They got together with a regiment of white-frocked gentlemen to cut me up.

When I was given the anesthetic, I was asked to count slowly—one, two, three, four . . .

I asked if instead I might repeat the Twenty-third Psalm.

The gentleman from Rochester nodded his assent, and the gentleman from London said, "Righto."

I began, "The Lord is my shepherd," and I can remember getting as far as "Thou art with me."

When I regained consciousness, I looked up to find that my benefactors were still there.

"Thank you," I said, "for helping me."

"It is you who have helped yourself and us," replied the Englishman, "because this operation we have performed without surgery is due only to the grace of God."

A person who has little or no faith might say, "Surely you don't think God sent one man across the ocean and another across the country to help you."

No, I do not. These men were to be at Johns Hopkins anyway.

But I do believe that God sent me to the table on the one day those men were scheduled to be at the hospital.

Then this person who has little faith might be expected to say, "You surely must rate yourself high in God's concern."

On the contrary, I rate myself very low. But the Bible tells us that God is no respecter of persons. We do not earn or deserve the love of God; we already have it.

It is His gift to us. We are born with it, and we die with it. No circumstance can take it away. All we need to take hold on it and to set it into operation is our faith.

God knows all of our needs before we take them to Him, but He tells us that we must ask if we are to receive. It is in humbling ourselves before Him and in asking that we lay bare our faith, and faith is the only power that will set into motion the cogs of the Spirit.

An experience such as I have just described—and there have been others—may explain why I have so much to say in the measly thirty minutes I am allotted each Lord's Day.

Now before we start the lesson of the day, I feel the need of adding a short footnote to the story I have just completed. The faith I have just described is not my sole possession. Indeed, I don't have enough for myself and surely not enough to spare any. But I have drunk at other wells, and I have been sustained day by day. Where I have drunk, you can drink, too.

All of this reminds me—naturally—of a story, the authenticity of which I can vouch for.

From out of the backwoods of Kentucky came a clod-hopping Romeo and his blushing Juliet to find a Justice of of the Peace. This good man would bind them in the holy bonds from which, the good Book says, there is no escape but death.

No sooner had the Justice, having successfully cleared his throat, begun the fateful reading than the wrathful father of the would-be bride made his noisy appearance.

An awesome verbal tempest followed. The frightened bride clung helplessly to the heaving bosom of her potato-growing protector.

"What does all this flapdoodle mean and what are you doing here?" roared the foaming father.

Whereupon the groom, in defense of his most honorable

intentions, shouted with equal vocal volume, "What others have did, we can do!"

There's a relation between Romeo's remark and the acquiring of faith, but I shall not belabor the point.

I cannot give you a faith by which you can live when your arms are elbow-deep in soap suds, when your child screams in danger, or when you pace the floor wondering why hubby hasn't come home yet. Neither can the Rector. Neither can anyone else. But God can give you such a faith, and He will. But you must be receptive. Knock and the door of faith will be opened unto you. But you have got to knock.

No one knows what God looks like. The Bible says that no man has ever looked upon the face of God and lived. Someday He will open a door for me that will never be closed. I just know that I will recognize Him, and I shall love Him at first sight. I am looking for that meeting in that Land that is fairer than day, as the hymn says, but, mind you, I'm in no special hurry. I've got a lot of closets in my mind to clear out first and some important tidying up to do.

When God sees me, I want to be dressed in my Sunday best, and I am not thinking only of my wardrobe.

Long ago at my father's country house I met one summer a remarkable woman whom we knew only as Miss Rose. She always wore upon her inflated bosom a crimson silk rose which was attached to a very long and curving rubber stem. She never neglected to drench said rose with lily-of-the-valley perfume. The combination of rose and perfume gave the nostrils an amazing surprise.

Equally surprising was her coiffure. Miss Rose regretfully admitted to having not a single hair on her head, but she turned this seeming misfortune into the delight of possessing three wigs. One was black and sleek. One was brown and windblown. Another was auburn with serpentine braids that coiled from bottom to top.

Miss Rose had classic features and skin like a magnolia petal. She truly could have worn anything on her head, but alas, she was a bird in a rusty small-town cage. Yet her hope of having it gilded and transported to far places was perpetual.

She had had three husbands—one for each wig. Now she had advertised for a fourth husband. To fire his ardor she had enclosed a picture of Mary Pickford.

When the enthusiastic would-be-mate arrived from the Texas Panhandle, he was bitterly disappointed. Miss Rose had neglected to add to her array of wigs one having long golden curls. What an oversight in one so adept at romance!

When I meet my Maker, I want to be sure that I am wearing the right wig. I don't want to lose out at the last moment because I don't have the right credentials.

Apropos of nothing in particular, except for my mentioning my sojourn at Johns Hopkins, is a story I want to tell so I won't forget it.

After I was released from the hospital early in December, I spent a few days with my daughter and four-year-old granddaughter at Washington. After some painful soul-searching and determined effort, I resolved that it was my grandmotherly responsibility to take Beverly into Woodward & Lothrop to see Santa Claus.

I thought it would give her a great thrill.

That was what I thought.

After climbing onto Santa's lap, Beverly put her tongue in her cheek, studied him closely with her large rolling eyes, and promptly expressed inappropriate disapproval.

Santa asked what she wanted for Christmas, and she informed him in no uncertain words that she was telling only grandmother what she wanted.

Santa was decidedly set back, and he showed both annoyance and chagrin, thereby indicating a lack of that priceless possession all Santas of my acquaintance had had, a sense of humor.

He hustled Beverly to the floor and ended the interview without any adieu. Another more gullible infant took his knee.

When we were trudging along the street once more, I waited for Beverly to make the first verbal move, but you could have cut through her silence.

So I said, "Didn't you like Santa Claus?"

She replied with a single word. "No."

"Why?" I asked.

"Because," she explained, "I don't trust anybody whose whiskers are tied on."

That night, after her prayers, which included Margaret Truman and the neighbor's white cat, Beverly asked me, "Grandmother, when I get to Heaven and sit on God's lap, will you be there?"

"I doubt it," I said—I sometimes have strange misgivings regarding my eligibility—and added, "There is a mighty lot of devilment in your old grandmother, and I am not sure St. Peter will let me in."

The possibility of grandmother's soul being incinerated in the Other Place was a matter of small or no importance to Beverly and was promptly disregarded.

Her mind was elsewhere.

Then she resolved her problem. "Well, if you are not there with me and God has His whiskers tied on, I'll tell you now, I'm leaving!"

When she said that, I am sure all of the angels in

Heaven were standing at the rail, looking down, and laughing angelically.

I think little children—even your own—are God's guideposts to His Kingdom.

What Beverly said was childish, but my remembrance of it shows that I have been able to retain through the years a modicum of childlikeness. There is a difference between childishness and childlikeness. If we are still childish when we enter our mature years, some kind men in white jackets will stop by and whisk us off to some safe place in order to protect society from our presence. If we retain a genuine childlikeness when we enter maturity, we shall never be hoodwinked by newspaper headlines or made sour by the "slings and arrows of outrageous fortune." The wonder, the faith, the trust, even the enthusiasm of small children ought not to be wasted on children. Is this not what Jesus meant when He said that if we do not "become as little children, ye shall not enter into the kingdom of heaven"?

If any one of us makes it to Heaven and then starts up with all of the pomposity, arrogance, and dull-eyed faith of grownups, he will surely be given a one-way ticket elsewhere, as happened to Lucifer.

We are all drifting on the stream of life toward one certain, inevitable, inescapable, and common goal, the grave. We all share one common hope, life everlasting.

The only time we have to live worthily is today, because one day at a time is all we ever have. Yesterday is gone, and tomorrow may never come. When we had yesterday, it was then today. If we are given tomorrow, when it comes, it too will be just today. Surely we can be trusted with life for just one day.

If you remember nothing else that I have said in class today, try to remember this. After life is over and done, there is absolutely nothing worth a darn except kindness.

When the course of our lives is run and we cross the finish line, if we have, in our running, bumped and hindered those alongside of us and made their going harder, although we may win, the victory will be ashes on our tongues.

We will find when the pay-off comes that the prize is counterfeit, and we will stand before God empty-handed, as spiritual paupers, having nothing of any value for ourselves or to offer Him.

Mine has been a varied life.

I have lived under four flags and have been closely associated with all manner and types and breeds of people.

I have dined in the homes of some of the wealthiest persons in the entire world, and I have squatted by torchlight to eat prison rations with a Georgia chain gang.

I have assisted a wife of the President of the United States at her garden parties, and I have nursed a harlot who was ill on shipboard.

I have stood at beds and assisted in the miracle of birth, and I have knelt at beds and offered comfort in the miracle of death and prayed for the dying with all the strength of my own good-for-nothing soul.

I have seen a proven embezzler of the pennies of widows and orphans go free in court, and I have helplessly witnessed a mob hanging an honest man.

I have taken up collections for the destitute and been given a pence by the rich and a pound by the poor.

I have traveled on velvet cushions by private car and now travel on the sharp tack of discomfort by bus.

After nearly sixty years of intensely diversified life to which it has evidently pleased God to call me, I have come to one ultimate and changeless conclusion. That being that some who call themselves Christians limit their piety to saying, "Lord, Lord," and some who feel unworthy of the name "Christian" incarnate in their words and actions all that makes the name of Christ great.

It is pathetically tragic that, with the exception of a handful who walked the earth with Jesus, so few have obeyed His voice.

After two thousand years, Christians have not yet given Christianity a real chance, because they have never practiced it as it was taught.

It is my firm, though insignificant, opinion that the destructive illness of the entire world could be completely cured by a single transfusion of the blood shed for all men, for all time, by a Nazarene upon a hilltop called Calvary.

Here endeth the lesson—which really never began.

Next Sunday I promise that memory will not interrupt the story of Ruth and Naomi.

Now our prayer. Again I ask you to close your eyes when praying. I do not say, "Bow your heads," for if I were to bow, my wide-brimmed hat would surely topple to the floor.

Virginia Comments on Alibis, Devilish Dan, and a Mother-in-Law

GOOD MORNING, SISTERS.

Today we honor fourteen women who have answered "Here" during our class roll call each Sunday during the past year. These women of holy habit offer a pious example for the rest of us. No doubt their lives are full and busy. Whereas the rest of us have weighed the pros and cons of attending each week—manipulating all of the last-minute duties and the aches and pains of our bodily nature against our obligation to be in our place each Sunday School period—these women have attended, like the proverbial postman on his rounds, come what may.

I have no doubt that many of those whose attendance has been spotty have had good reasons for being away. Church members have the most remarkable excuses in all the world. I don't need to read off the best alibis—I know them all by heart from past experience—but once in a while a new one turns up which I wish I had thought of myself.

70

Example one: "I awakened with such a smashing headache that I thought it would be better to die peacefully in my own bed at home than to cause confusion in the House of the Lord."

Example two: "My husband had to go out of town on a business trip, and I forgot to ask him for money for the class collection. So, of course, I couldn't come."

Example three: "The children had been rambunctious all week long. I knew they would have to be disciplined, but I kept putting it off. The first chance I had was Sunday morning. So instead of Sunday School, I kept them home and put the fear of God in them myself."

Example four: "The Rector's wife didn't speak to me last week, and so I decided not to listen to him for an hour on Sunday."

The other day one of our own members phoned to explain her absence on a particular Sunday. Her explanation was routine. I explained that she need not offer any reason to me. "As far as I am concerned, the Lord keeps the books, not I," I said in my number one consoling voice.

"But, Miss Virginia, I called to say that I hope I didn't miss anything important."

"Not a thing," I replied.

I suppose the fourteen women who got the perfect attendance pins today have the capacity of doing whatever has got to be done. Some people are like that. They do twice as much as the next person, and they are never hot and bothered. They have a God-given gift denied to others.

Before the Brown Hotel in Louisville stands a figure worthy of the contemplation of all mankind. The Perennial Doorman. Ever alert, always polite, he advances and retreats, slides and glides, and opens and closes the automobile doors of a nation.

With the grace of a ballet master and the regal manner of a lord, this creature of elegance, in his spotless livery and gleaming buttons, awaits your bidding twenty-four hours of every day.

After observing this phenomenon year after year, I finally accosted him in real earnestness of purpose to learn how he managed to stand at his post day and night without rest or relief from duty.

With a gracious Brummel bow that would surely have shamed even the old Beau himself, he divulged his secret. "I manage just fine, Ma'am," he said. "You see, I is twins!"

Our lesson today is about Naomi, not Ruth—we'll leave her on her pedestal—but talk about Ruth's mother-in-law, who has never gotten the attention she deserves. This shortcoming I intend to rectify this morning.

First, however, I want to tell you an old timey story that I almost forgot I knew until a few days ago when Barbara Bartlett, the mother of two of our class members, and I got to putting flesh on old skeletons. Then I remembered Devilish Dan.

Ma Bartlett insisted that I tell his story to her daughters.

"Well, I see them every Sunday in the Deborah Class," I said.

"Well, I'll tell them to insist that you tell them about Devilish Dan," Ma commented.

"That won't be necessary," I replied. "I've got a captive audience, I decide what the lesson will be, and someday I'll use Devilish Dan as a filler. Devilish Dan would love me for it anyway."

That "someday" is right now.

Devilish Dan, as I call him half in jest and half in earnest, was so called because he was so full of the devil.

I won't tell you his real name because some of his kinsmen are still hereabouts, and they are upright church-people of quality and grace.

I knew Devilish Dan nearly forty years ago. I would see him summers when I went to auntie's country house overlooking the river.

He was decidedly the most colorful character I have ever known. To pass a summer afternoon, I would drive to town and persuade him to come and drink lemonade with me under the trees.

He was the cutest old man, and I just loved him. He lived to be nearly one hundred, and I remember how he squeaked and creaked with age.

I found him to be the most diverting and delightfully entertaining liar I have ever been privileged to swap stories with.

He was, as the people there said, "on speaking terms with ghosts and demons." He was a rabid spiritualist. The departed got through to him with the most fantastic messages imaginable. His close contact with and intimate knowledge of spooks would have made Conan Doyle a bush-leaguer. All of his life Devilish Dan had been a human magnet attracting the unusual. When I was with him, the happenings in the actual world seemed like fabricated myths.

An invisible Indian maiden followed him everywhere he went and gave him advice. Of course, she was invisible to me, because I had no clairvoyant talent and was a disbeliever. But she was often included by him in our conversations when we sat beneath the persimmon trees and sipped lemonades. Her ad-libs, which Devilish Dan translated for me, made me feel that she was kind of cute. I felt that my failure to visualize her was my loss.

In those days many shanty boats plied the river. One

was built like an ark. On its side was a large sign reading "The White Dove." On board was a buxom blonde crystal gazer, palmist, and medium of indeterminate age.

This female mystic was bone of Devilish Dan's bone and flesh of his flesh.

One day she told him to hurry to the general store. On the candy counter he would find two stacks of Louisiana Lottery tickets. He was to count down on the lefthand pile and take the seventh ticket from the bottom.

Devilish Dan bought the ticket, won the lottery, and got himself a good river-bottom farm.

When "The White Dove" drifted downstream the following year, Devilish Dan was on the gangplank a few minutes after it came to a resting place in the wet gravel. He greeted the blonde mystic by placing a thousand dollar bill in her palm.

She in turn told him that the spirits could see a horse race and winning it was a bay having four white feet and the only horse shipped in from the East.

Ah! he thought, the Derby! And that very week!

Well, over the protestations of his banker, Mr. Whitman, and in spite of the tears of his wife, old Devilish Dan mortgaged his farm for ten thousand, left Davenport on the five a.m. Derby train, and adorned in his tall hat and his heavy gold watch chain dangling heavy with many mystic charms, he went to Churchill Downs, where he strolled from barn to barn until he found a bay having four white feet and just shipped in from the East.

Now Devilish Dan was not by nature a gambler, but the spirits, who were all-knowing, couldn't be wrong. Besides, the Indian maiden kept nudging him on.

The horse closed at ten to one.

Shortly before midnight the St. Louis-bound Cannon Ball stopped at Davenport for coal and water. Devilish

Dan hit the platform with a new bounce in his old feet. His newly found fortune was pinned with safety pins to his underwear. He dried his wife's tears with diamond ear-bobs, a seal coat which reached to her heels, a bearskin carriage robe, and a house in town.

"What happened to 'The White Dove' and your mystic friend," I asked Devilish Dan at least a dozen times.

His answer was always the same. "The boat's at the bottom of the river somewhere, and my little dove bought a house and orange grove in Florida with the five thousand I gave her."

When I knew Devilish Dan, all he had left were the Indian maiden and his spirit world.

Some lingering compassion for the human race persuaded me to divert enough money from the Lord's tithe to purchase a two-way train ticket so that Devilish Dan might go to Locust Valley where the spiritualists were holding a meeting for all believers in the unbelievable and visionists of the invisible. Old Dan was so pleased that he jumped rope while dancing the jig, and he promised to bequeath to me the ever-present Indian maiden when he should journey on to his true habitation, which came all too soon.

If I might keep Naomi waiting for a moment or two, I should like to tell you about a secret and investigative sympathizer of all things spiritual and spooky, who went to the same Locust Valley meetings each year.

He was the town dentist, whom I shall call Dr. C. His interest had been aroused to action by rappings heard in his attic by none other than himself.

Dr. C. was a soft-spoken, pussy-footing, and fragrantly-scented gentleman, who was forever patting a skin freshener on his thin and haggard jowls.

One day when I was seated in his dentist chair and

inhaling and exhaling his skin freshener, his wife, who was ironically named Charity, stormed in. There before my astonished eyes, she so successfully brandished a tennis racket as to reduce Dr. C. to a whimpering suppliant.

Knowing that she had borne him six children in five years, I figured that he had it coming to him. So I just sat it out.

Between her ravings, I gathered that she had discovered, at that very hour, a photograph which he had brought back from the spiritualists' jamboree. In her rage Mrs. C. thrust the photograph into my hands. The photograph showed Dr. C. all right and in a most blissful pose.

What got Mrs. C. so upset was that behind him in the picture was the likeness of his dear, dead first wife, her cheek pressed tenderly against his own. Perhaps she had returned for just one more whiff and sniff of his favorite skin freshener.

I suppose it might be just as well if you promise not to pass along to the Rector these uplifting little moral tales. I would not want that there should be any misunderstandings.

Our lesson today is from the Book of Ruth, which should have been called the Book of Naomi, because, while the role of Ruth is largely passive, it is Naomi whose wisdom, generosity, and goodness initiates and brings to a satisfying conclusion almost everything worthwhile in this extraordinarily beautiful and inspiring story.

The bewhiskered old men who write the Bible commentaries don't tell you what I am going to say this morning. You go home and read this short book and then let me know if I am not more right than they.

In the midst of all of the blood and thunder of Hebrew history we come upon this little book in which absolutely no one hates or fights or distrusts anyone else. Everything here is peace and love and quiet contentment, which shows that man does not live by battles and strife only. This book is like the silence between the heaves of storm. Blessed silence!

When the story opens we find Naomi, a native of Bethlehem, living in Moab. Why she is in Moab we are not told. No doubt a drought in the Promised Land had driven Bethlehemites into other countries, even as a drought had sent the family of Jacob to Egypt.

Naomi's husband, Elimelech, has died. Her two sons, Mahlon and Chilion, after marrying Moabite maidens, named Orpah and Ruth respectively, have also died.

So what do we now have left? A widow and her widowed daughters-in-law, a most unlikely situation for a story of peace and harmony!

In time Naomi hears that the grass in Bethlehem is green once more, and she decides that it is time for her to return to her own people. She tells Orpah and Ruth one morning after breakfast of her plans. They must, she says, return to their people and she to hers.

Orpah thinks the plan is a good one, but Ruth does not want to be parted from her mother-in-law.

"Go your way," Naomi insists.

But Ruth is recalcitrant. In some of the most beautiful words in the whole Bible, Ruth pleads:

> Entreat me not to leave thee, or to return from following after thee: for whither thou goest, I will go; and where thou lodgest, I will lodge: thy people shall be my people, and thy God my God: where thou diest, will I die, and there will I be buried: the Lord do so to me, and more also, if aught but death part thee and me.

We are told repeatedly that this is a matchless example of sacrificial love.

And so it is.

We are told that nowhere, except perhaps for Jonathan's expression of friendship for David, are we likely to find a finer testimony of friendship.

And this is true.

Yet we must not overlook the person to whom Ruth made this plea and why.

Perhaps Ruth had no people of her own to return to. Perhaps only in the presence of Naomi was the memory of her dead husband radiant and beautiful. Who knows?

We do know that Naomi was the kind of person who solicits such a plea. And we know that when Naomi was persuaded by Ruth's eloquent pleas, she assumed a personal responsibility for Ruth's welfare which might well have been beyond her means.

When Naomi said yes, Ruth was the only person who really benefited.

So Naomi and her devoted daughter-in-law returned to Bethlehem, where Ruth would have been at a loss among those whose customs were strange to her and whose language she could speak only falteringly. But Naomi knew her way about town. She looked over the situation and concluded that her kinsman, a middle-aged bachelor named Boaz, was the most likely matrimonial prospect. Naomi then told Ruth to glean in the harvest fields belonging to Boaz. There she would surely be noticed.

And, of course, she was—by Boaz.

He asked whom she might be, and he learned that she was related to him by marriage. He told Ruth to glean only in his fields, and this she dutifully reported to Naomi.

When the time seemed right, Naomi told Ruth:

> Wash thy self therefore, and anoint thee, and put thy raiment upon thee, and get thee down to the [threshing] floor: but make not thyself known unto

the man, until he shall have done eating and drinking.

And it shall be, when he lieth down, that thou shalt mark the place where he shall lie, and thou shalt go in, and uncover his feet, and lay thee down; and he will tell thee what thou shalt do.

Ruth acquiesced, saying, "All that thou sayest unto me I will do."

Naomi knew what she was up to, and Boaz took the bait she offered.

As a result Boaz and Ruth were married, and in time to them was born a son named Obed. "And Naomi took the child, and laid it in her bosom, and became nurse unto it."

Naomi was satisfied. Ruth would be cared for when Naomi's days came to an end. She had repaid Ruth for her tender love and concern.

Obed descendants included Jesse, David, Solomon, and our Lord Jesus.

The Book of Ruth was not, however, written to extol the virtues of Naomi. Rather, the writer rose above the popular outcry of his generation against foreigners to say something like this, "Wait, now, the greatest of the worthies of our race have come from the hands of a daughter of the Moabites."

This priceless story has a message for us. The moral of this book has not yet gotten through to us. We have yet to learn that God is no respecter of persons.

All human beings are God's children, and we are their brothers and sisters in Christ. We ought to begin to behave this way.

All Christians belong to the Body of Christ, and whatever their creed or denomination, they are members of one Household of Faith. We ought to begin to behave as though this is true.

What men everywhere have not yet learned is that the Church of Christ belongs to Christ and not to men. In His love and in His teaching there is no division.

Let us not wedge ourselves into a hopeless deadlock by wasting our time in comparing what we believe with what others believe. We must return to the Testaments for a common source of belief.

I am skeptical of all the ecumenical varnish that is being spread by men who speak high-sounding words. The world will detect a note of insincerity when on the one hand we talk enthusiastically about unity and then on the other hand act directly to the contrary.

The Word of God strips all men of their personal treasure of national, social, political, and cultural self-assurance and self-complacency. These weapons which we use to defend our portion of truth will at the end leave us standing naked before our Maker.

There was born in Sweden toward the end of the seventeenth century one Emanuel Swedenborg, who when he came to maturity devoted himself to the studies of mathematics and mechanics.

He was a practical and successful scientist, whose proficiency brought him into the intimate and unbounded confidence of Charles XII. He was neither a fanatic nor a screwball promoter. His reputation was universally established as being the most profound thinker of his age.

When Swedenborg was fifty-seven, he went before his King and said: "My previous studies have served their purpose. I shall devote the remainder of my days to the study of the Sacred Scriptures. Having been called to a new and holy office, the Lord has granted me sight to view a spiritual world and afforded me the privilege to converse with spirits and angels."

But before you say, "Oh, another Devilish Dan," let

me remind you of the visions and voices seen and heard by Moses, Jacob, Samuel, Joseph, Paul, Joan of Arc, and many another. God has many things to show and tell us, but we are too occupied in our own private, puny, and everlastingly important affairs.

When I was fifteen years old, Bishop Jordan required his class in Christian education to read Swedenborg's *True Christian Religion*. Its impression has outlasted the years. I remember it as a dramatic and sweeping appeal to all men who would be followers of—not only believers in— Jesus Christ.

This Swedenborg, genuinely distressed over church division, sounded the clarion call of all true ecumenicalists. He waged a one-man crusade to bring spiritual order out of religious chaos.

I know that the name of Swedenborg has been largely forgotten. What does that matter? The important thing is that his ideas should be remembered.

God does not look down upon us for our religious nameplate or creed. He seeks a place in our hearts, and He looks for some manifestation of Himself in our daily lives. Christians, alas, have not yet fully comprehended the universal love of God. Yet, thank God, there are some individuals within the churches who have received the inner benediction of His spiritual vision. I pray God that you and I may be counted among them.

I hope you have not been wearied beyond repair by my testimony.

I trust the Lord will restore your souls during our closing prayer.

Virginia Enlarges the Bible and Extols Patriotism

BELOVED SISTERS.

I have brought along to class this morning a personal item of no commercial value but of inestimable sentimental value to me. But before I show it to you, there is a little story centering in it. I don't know whether I have brought this particular item so that I might thereby have an excuse to tell the story or whether I shall tell the story for the purpose of passing around among you this item.

At any rate, I trust my mysterious manner has whetted your interest.

Always in the fall of my earlier years my father's friends would congregate from near and far at the country house which was located on a high cliff overlooking a perfect horseshoe bend of the Ohio River. I have mentioned this country house on previous Sundays.

Fall included "the hunting season," and my father's friends comprised an annual hunting party.

A week or two in advance of their arrival I drove down with the necessary provisions and supplies. Then after the men had gathered in all beast and fowl within range of their rifles, I would return to close up for the winter.

One particular year, after the last leaf had fallen and the last house guest had returned to the city, I braved the brisk winds to do the closing-up chores.

I was surprised to find the front door open. I saw immediately that the lock had been forcibly removed. When I entered the living room, my surprise was transformed to speechless shock. The room was in an unbelievably chaotic condition. Cushions had been pulled from upturned chairs. Pictures had been torn from the walls. Books had been shoved from the shelves. Rugs had been tossed into a corner.

In father's bedroom the sheets had been torn from the bed. The dresser drawers had been ransacked and their contents removed. The handsome hunting clothes were gone, as were the guns which father's friends always left behind for use the following year.

The pattern was the same in room after room. Silver, linen, kitchenware—all were gone.

Thunderstruck, I then opened the door to my bedroom. Sunlight, streaming through the window, illuminated a large mother-of-pearl cross which I had long before hung on the side wall. Beneath this cross was a large knapsack which had been made from sheets ripped from the various beds.

I immediately sensed what had happened. The intruder had entered the room when the sun illuminated the cross. That cross had conveyed some message to the thief. I do not know what the cross meant to him or what memories it kindled in his mind. All I know is that beneath the cross he had unloaded his burden, each and every thing taken being accounted for.

Having told this story, I want to pass among you this same mother-of-pearl cross. In itself this cross possesses no miraculous power for protecting your houses from forced entry or for accomplishing any other feat. But this cross—or any cross of whatever size and shape—serves to remind us, as it apparently did for the thief, that at the heart of life is divine love and sacrifice.

Today, being Missionary Sunday, we are particularly reminded of the compelling power of the Cross, which has meant so much to some people that they have forsaken all of the comforts and companions at home in order to take the Cross into the homes of needy people living at the four corners of this earth.

The mission field has been acknowledged as the harvest field of God.

I have known personally some outstanding missionaries. A dear friend of my mother spent fifty years in Japan. A cousin of my husband lived for forty years in China. There were others who stopped at our home when I was a child and later.

I find most public lectures by missionaries to be routine. I like the pictures well enough, but the missionary is usually so on edge for fear he will say something that will provoke the displeasure of those he hopes to please that he hesitates before and after each word he utters. When he completes his message, which should be the very heartbeat of Christianity, everyone claps, a few give, and most of the listeners forget what he has not dared to say.

Then later, if you can get him in a corner and warm him up over a cup of coffee, he will tell you freely and frankly why he cannot accomplish what our Lord commissioned him to do. The trouble lies in denominational rivalry.

When you probe, you know what he will say before he speaks—that the people with whom he labors have difficulty grasping the differing interpretations of the same faith.

Then you ask, "Why don't you boys get together and tell them the same story?"

Well, he thinks it is about time he should be going, and you fully agree with him. He gathers up his disappointingly meager funds, sails over the bounding deep, and resumes his flapdoodle rivalry which he knows is confusing to the people he serves. They come to him for medicine, food, and learning, and then return to their own temples to pray.

And you too continue to be confused, but you seal your dollar in the mission side of your envelope, hoping that it may do more good than you expect it to.

Not until Christian people get together in one common endeavor will the full Harvest of God be reaped.

God is our Father, and we are His children. Our bloodline is greater than our particular creeds, positions, or wealth. When in unity we pour our hearts and souls into practicing what we preach, then, and only then, can our example hope to Christianize the world.

Do my words sound too doleful? I hope deep in my heart that I am wrong, but in my head I know I speak truthfully. I have not spoken with all of our missionaries, but the dozen or so I know bear me witness.

In regard to this, I find the Rector and I to be in one hundred per cent harmony. Three or four years ago he told me that he felt so strongly about this that he was going to preach a pulpit-thumping sermon on the subject. Perhaps that will be his topic today.

But that is up to him, and what I talk about in this class is up to me. My topic today concerns a woman who is and is not a Bible character. She is in our family Bible at home, but you won't find her name in the Bible I bring to class.

Don't think I'm playing a game with you. The woman in question is Judith, and the book bearing her name is in the Apocrypha.

The various stories and precepts in the fourteen or fifteen books of the Apocrypha should be known to all Christians. These books fill the blank page between Malachi and Matthew. They tell us what the Jews were doing and thinking during the long centuries between the prophets and Him whom the prophets foretold. They represent the bridge between the Testaments.

The men who gave us the King James Version considered the Apocrypha to be edifying for the faithful, and they did themselves a proud job in their translation of the Apocrypha.

But Mr. Luther and Mr. Calvin, among others, questioned the value of these books, and I am not now prepared to question their judgment regarding this. They did not believe these books to represent God's Word.

So the Book of Judith is not found in most Protestant Bibles. In order to make sure I would be on safe ground, I crept into the pulpit after church last Sunday to take a look at the Rector's monstrous Bible. He was in the vestibule listening to the old ladies tell him how good his sermon was, and I knew he would not catch me.

What did I find in that pulpit? A glass of water—undrunk. A roll of Life Savers—untouched. Several Kleenex —unused. A beautifully typed sermon with all the pressure points marked boldly in blue penciling. And the Apocrypha between the Old and New Testaments—in small type.

Later when I sought the Rector's judgment on the Book of Judith, he allowed that the book lacked historicity. I was real proud of the way he said "historicity." I knew right away why two colleges had conferred upon him those beautiful mufflers and the D.D.'s.

Of course, anything that has not got historicity is not worth a darn. That's why Hamlet never quite made it and why the cherry tree got chopped down in the backyard of the Washington home.

Once there lived in a very small Ohio River town an unlettered yet knowing woman named Annie, who resided with her liquor-consuming son and his gum-chewing wife, who had multiplied and replenished until the very walls rang with colic, croup, shrieks, and wails.

Among these numerous offspring was Annie's namesake, the darling of her heart, who by special request was called Anna. Annie thought Anna sounded more ladylike than Annie.

One day Anna fled home from school into the ever-waiting arms of her grandmother and buried her small tear-drenched face against Annie's calico-clad bosom. Gathering the grief-stricken form into her lap, she waited for the sobbing to cease.

"Grandmammy," sniffed Anna, catching her breath, "teacher says I can't pass 'cause I don't know no history."

"Shucks!" snorted the mystified, indignant Annie, who rocked fiercely in her squeaking chair. Forthwith came the following much-worth-remembering advice: "Don't you cry, child, as long as you live about no history, and your grandmammy is telling you now that history ain't nothing but just a lot of old hearsay!"

History or only hearsay, the story of Judith is well worth reading and remembering. The story is too good not to be true. Besides, there is a good deal of untrue truth that is true in its own way.

For instance, I have long kept in my Bible—the one that did not make room for Judith—a tattered newspaper clipping that purports to give a description of "the true likeness of our Savior." The paper makes this claim: "This description of the person of our Savior is taken from a manuscript now in the possession of a peer of the realm, and in his library, and was copied from the original letter of Publius Lentullus at Rome."

The description reads as follows:

> There appeared in these our days a man of great virtue, named Jesus Christ, who is yet living among us, and of the Gentiles is accepted for a Prophet of Truth, but his own disciples call him the Son of God. He raiseth the dead and cureth all manner of disease.
>
> A man of stature somewhat tall and comely, with very reverend countenance, such as the beholders may both love and fear—his hair of the colour of chestnut full ripe, plain to his ears, whence downward it is more orient and curling and wavering about his shoulders; in the midst of his head is a seam or partition in his hair, after the manner of the Nazarites.
>
> His forehead plain and very delicate, his face without spot or wrinkle, beautiful with a lovely red—his nose and mouth so formed as nothing can be reprehended, his beard thickish, in colour like his hair—not very long but forked, his look innocent and mature, his eyes grey, clear and quick. In reproving he is terrible, in admonishing, courteous and fair spoken, pleasant in conversation, mixed with gravity. It cannot be remembered that any have seen him laugh, but many have seen him weep. In proportion of body excellent, his hands and arms most delicate to behold. In speaking very temperate, modest and wise. A man for his singular beauty, surpassing the children of men.

Now I know that this description is not "historicity," but I love it. When the Golden Gates are opened wide—and they will have to be opened wide if I am ever to squeeze through!—I shall have no trouble at all in recognizing my Savior. I only hope that by His grace I may be recognized by Him! But on that day I admit I shall be disappointed if He does not resemble the description I have just read.

By the way, if any of you want a copy of this description, I will be more than pleased to give it to you.

Judith was a woman of extraordinary beauty—the Helen of Troy of Hebrew history. She lived at the time when Nebuchadnezzar's army was ravishing all things Jewish, and one of his more ruthless and successful generals, a pompous and conceited ass named Holofernes, had set up a siege around Bethulia, Judith's hometown, and he cut off their water supply. In time the situation became desperate, and the city fathers agreed to surrender their life and liberty in five days if divine intervention was not forthcoming.

Judith, a young, wealthy, and pious widow, had separated herself from the affairs of her people after her husband Manasseh died of sunstroke three years previously. Adorned in sackcloth, she perpetuated her grief interminably and gave herself to prayer and fasting.

When, however, word of the faithlessness of the people came to her ears, she reprimanded the leaders, offered one of the most genuine prayers you are likely to find anywhere, and prepared to do battle in the only way open to her.

I shall permit the unknown writer of her story to tell of her unusual stratagem:

> She . . . pulled off the sackcloth which she had on, and put off the garments of her widowhood, and washed her body all over with water, and anointed herself with precious ointment, and braided the hair

of her head, and put on a tire upon it, and put on her garments of gladness, wherewith she was clad during the life of Manasseh her husband.

And she took sandals upon her feet, and put about her her bracelets, and her chains, and her rings, and her earrings, and all her ornaments, and decked herself bravely, to allure the eyes of all men that should see her.

Then she gave her maid a bottle of wine, and a cruse of oil, and filled a bag with parched corn, and lumps of figs, and with fine bread; so she folded all these things together, and laid them upon her.

Then Judith and her attendant passed through the gates of Bethulia, crossed the valley, and were confronted by the Assyrian guard to whom Judith told of the faithlessness of her people and of their forthcoming defeat.

One hundred of the enemy tumbled over one another to escort Judith to the tent of Holofernes, for "they wondered at her beauty, and admired the children of Israel because of her, and every one said to his neighbor, Who would despise this people, that have among them such women?"

General Holofernes, who "rested upon his bed under a canopy, which was woven with purple, and gold, and emeralds, and precious stones," became as giddy as the enlisted men. So taken was he by her beauty that he took in her story, hook, line, and sinker.

She asked only that she and her maiden might leave the camp each night for prayers and to partake of the kosher food in her tote bag. Holofernes, who greedily waited for the time when he might have her to himself, offered every conceivable concession to Judith.

That opportunity came on the fourth day, when Holofernes had a feast brought into his tent and all of his men put out. Sick with desire, Holofernes said to his lone companion, "Drink now, and be merry with us."

So elated was Holofernes that he "drank much more wine than he had drunk at any time in one day since he was born."

By nightfall Holofernes was out cold on his canopied bed, and Judith fulfilled her mission by separating his head from his body by using his ever-ready sword.

Judith put the head into her tote bag—she would need proof because no one back home was likely to believe her —passed from the tent, picked up her faithful maid, and bade good evening to the goggle-eyed guards, who thought she was merely retiring for her customary prayers.

Back in Bethulia the faithless leaders of God's people found their faith renewed, marveled at what God had accomplished "by the hand of a woman," and in the morning hanged the head of Holofernes upon the wall of the city.

Needless to say, when the hordes of the Assyrians learned what had happened, "fear and trembling fell upon them," and they fled like scared rabbits.

Judith now returned to her own house, where she engaged again in mourning for her long-dead husband.

Now, good Sisters, I do not commend Judith's actions to you, although her devotion to God and her ardent patriotism are commendable beyond compare.

God has often brought about His glory "by the hand of a woman." Barak, you remember, would not do battle for the Lord until Deborah promised to go with him. Jael became a savior of the Hebrews when she drove a tent peg through the skull of the unsuspecting Sisera. After she finally put aside her own self-concern, Esther realized that she had "come to the kingdom for such a time as this," and she frustrated the plans of Haman to destroy her people.

In a day when too many people speak of God only in whispers and seem embarrassed by the word "patriotism," it is high time that women engage in a vigorous spiritual warfare in behalf of liberty and faith.

Most of us are not endowed with the matchless beauty of Judith, but whatever talent we have we must use in our community, our home, and our church.

The blood of heroes and martyrs flows through our veins. Our Lord bequeathed to us a legacy of soul freedom. George Washington bequeathed to us a heritage of physical freedom.

Freedom of body and soul are inseparable. Washington's men did not know him as the man having the most gold braid. They knew him as the one among them who, at every sunrise, sank on his knees to thank Almighty God for His protection in all things past and to ask His guidance in all things to come.

Can we do less?

Now with these stirring words ringing in your ears, let us restore ourselves to the Throne of Grace for prayer.

Virginia Berates Bible Commentators and Talks of Angels

SISTER DEBORAHITES.

This morning I'm going on strike against all of the riga-marole that clutters the beginning of our class. Most of the notes, notices, announcements, and reminders of this and that are pretty nonsensical anyway.

How's a poor old teacher to teach a lesson if she is expected to be dispatcher of every caboose that leaves the church freight yard?

First, there's the humiliating report on last Sunday's collection. (Last Sunday, by the way, we took in twenty dollars and eighty cents or on average thirty-two cents for each woman attending. That shows some improvement, but I don't hear any angels applauding. Thirty-two cents won't put rice in many bowls. And that's our Christian obligation. To put rice in the bowls of hungry children around the world. Rice in their empty bowls and the love of a merciful God in their empty hearts. All else is super-ficial according to the way I read the Book.)

Second, there are the church announcements.

"Prayer and Sermon at eleven." Eleven is always under-scored. Prayer and Sermon is always at eleven. Even the devil couldn't find a better hour! I suppose the underscoring is a not-too-subtle suggestion that I bring the lesson to a close in time for Prayer and Sermon at eleven. Which I have always faithfully done.

"And please remember to announce the Rector's sermon title."

Today it is "Peace." I presume the text will be John Fourteen Twenty-seven. There will be three points:

ONE. No peace in the world.

TWO. The peace Christ offers.

THREE. How to find peace for yourself.

Several pious and profane authors will be quoted, and for want of anything better, the sermon will close with a mournful recitation of "Peace, perfect peace, in this dark world of sin." Then we will all quietly pass out.

Almost any Sunday I'm asked to read the church calendar of "Work in the Vineyard." The little kids party, the not-so-little kids party, the not-so-big kids party, the big kids party, and the mothers-of-kids party will be held heaven only knows when or where or why. And Circles One through Twenty-one will hold their regular monthly sewing meetings one week late this month at the regular times and places. And the St. Matthew Men's Bowling League will meet on Tuesday, the Bishop's Spiritual Investment Group on Wednesday, and the Galilean Yachting Club on Friday. Besides, there is a pancake supper on Monday, a fellowship dinner on Wednesday, a fish fry on Saturday, and committee meetings in between. Additionally, the church is open for meditation every weekday from eight to five, and, of course, the Quiet Hour Service is held from twelve-fifty p.m. to one p.m. daily except Wednesdays.

"And please don't forget to announce that the six choirs

will rehearse at their regular times. Choir members know all about this."

Third, there are all of the financial concerns. Please give to the Lamplight Mission, the Bishop's Rescue Research Fund, the Beckoning Beacon Home, and the Holiness Guide Guild.

Fourth, I am asked to berate the faithful who always attend for the nonattendance in Sunday School of those who couldn't care less. "A year ago—" or "Our goal this year—" So please come and I'll not mention the subject again.

My main reason for foregoing the usual announcements today is that I need the time to turn to that woman who among all of the women in the Bible has always claimed the particular love and esteem of mankind.

I refer, of course, to Mary of Nazareth, who is the mother of our Lord.

To think about Mary is to move from a dusty road into a rose garden, to climb from low valleys to mountaintops, to leave the hubbub and turmoil of a topsy-turvy world and enter into the beauty, serenity, and peace of a wayside chapel.

A good and godly man named Simeon said to Mary, "Yea, a sword shall pierce through thy own soul also."

The sword of Golgotha pierced her soul. Misunderstandings within the Nazareth family caused heartbreak. But surely the greatest pain of all must have come through the contentions and confusions, the bickering and quarreling, of estimable churchmen during the past two thousand years concerning the simple role which God gave to this guileless young woman to play in His cosmic plan of redemption.

I have turned from one commentary to another. What

do I read? All kinds of assertions, arguments, and refutations about Mary.

Why don't the esteemed theologians see what the Bible with exquisite simplicity has to say regarding her? Why don't they humbly accept the words which the Bible offers?

But I don't expect they will—not ever.

So perhaps it is up to us to cut through the theological fat and find the true picture.

And perhaps only a mother can ever really know Mary and share her glorious experience, for, above all else, Mary is for us all that is true and good and beautiful in motherhood.

Words like the Virgin Mary remove Mary from us, creating a gulf between her motherhood and our motherhood. Actually, we should feel very close to her. Were she to join our class this morning, she would not seem strange to us. We would sense her sincerity, her devotion to God, and her winsome love and loveliness. We would feel the warmth of her companionship and the inspiration of her being among us. But we would not hesitate to speak with her about all of those trivial matters that are so important to mothers. Nor would we feel uncomfortable in her presence.

Yet Mary, by God's own choice, walks in a circle of light which is denied to us. For Mary shared in a co-partnership with God in a parenthood that was destined to save and to bless mankind through an Incarnation of Light and Life and Love. To the extent that Jesus is the unique revealing of the heart of God, Mary knew a motherhood that is unique among all women.

The story of Mary is woven on a loom whose warp is Biblical fact and whose woof is pious legend and lore. Perhaps with a well-harnessed imagination we can recite her story according to the following fashion.

Mary was born in the town of Nazareth on September 8 about nineteen years before the birth of our Lord and some twenty-nine or thirty years after that of the man who was to become her husband.

How can I be so precise about all this? Well, I can't be. But then the dates and places come from my reading and not out of my own head.

Her parents are described as "pious and well-stricken in years." Anna, her mother, was of the house of David. Joachim, her father, was a priest having religious duties in their hometown of Nazareth. He was of the tribe of Aaron, a people set apart by God to minister to Him as priests.

All kinds of fanciful legends relate the story of Mary's childhood and girlhood. Some are farfetched and others encourage credulity. All are fashioned to honor a woman whose choice by God makes everything else pale by comparison.

That she was exemplary in manner and deportment goes without question. That she was devout and God-fearing would have been essential for the fulfillment of God's purpose. That among all Jewish women of that time and generation—or indeed of our time and generation—there were not others of equal poise and piety would be hard for me to believe.

In every period of history, thank God! there have been good and gracious women whom God has singled out for particular purposes.

Yet Mary was the one among tens of thousands who was chosen by God to be the mother of our Lord.

In the same town of Nazareth lived a man named Joseph. Tradition says he was about fifty when God put him into the Gospel story. Whether this tradition is right or wrong, I do not know. His age doesn't much matter, although there seems to be considerable support—I don't know why

—for believing he was much older than Mary. Perhaps it is only my femininity which makes me want to picture him as young, strong, and probably handsome!

Joseph is identified as a carpenter by trade. But to call him only a carpenter would be like calling Michelangelo a house painter because he painted the walls of the Sistine Chapel.

Joseph did not shoulder a ladder, shuffle among wood shavings, and bang on boards. Rather was he an artisan of fine woods and precious metals. He was a master damascene. Damascening is the art of applying one metal upon another in intricate and ornate designs. This costly and elaborate service was rendered to the generals of the armies of Israel and was confined usually to the handles of swords and breastplates.

Is this something you haven't heard before? Well, that is why you come to Sunday School.

Joseph was of the tribe of Judah. St. Matthew, whose Gospel was written from the point of view of Joseph, traces his lineage from David through Solomon. St. Luke, writing from the point of view of Mary, traces the same lineage through Nathan.

This seeming contradiction is in reality only a complication. Jacob and Eli were brothers. Eli, dying without issue, gave his wife to his brother Jacob by whom she bore Joseph. Under Mosiac law, therefore, Joseph was the son of Eli, while under natural law, he was the son of Jacob.

Into the routine pattern of Mary's life and into Joseph's workaday world came divine messengers with the most startling announcements. I do not know whether the same angel appeared to both Mary and Joseph. I rather suspect that God has legions of angels who even today bear His messages and that God's will is mediated in ways that far outdistance our understanding.

Mary seems not to have been startled by the appearance of the angel Gabriel.

You could explain this with a shrug of the shoulder and the comment that, after all, Mary was young and naïve and lived in a less sophisticated age than ours. Or you could say that there were angels in those days, but there aren't any around today.

But such explanations don't explain anything.

Mary was a woman who was sensitive to the will and way of God. Her heart was tuned in. God was very real to her. Her love of God knew no bounds. She just naturally expected that God communicated with His children.

Gabriel said to Mary, "Hail, thou that art highly favoured, the Lord is with thee: blessed art thou among women."

These words "troubled" Mary. Why? Because the angel had shown preference for her over other women, and Mary, who was modest and humble, knew in her own heart that she was unworthy. That is the manner of all truly humble persons.

So Gabriel reassures her. "Fear not, Mary: for thou hast found favour with God." Then he explains the unexplainable and concludes by saying, "For with God nothing shall be impossible."

What does Mary say to all this?

"My mind is playing tricks on me." No, this possibility doesn't cross her mind.

"You must have the wrong address." No, she knew the message was for her.

"I am unable and unwilling to do what God asks." No, she accepts the assignment.

When God called Noah, he tried to excuse himself.

When God called Moses, he supported his refusal by listing his deficiencies.

102

When God called Saul, he went and hid.

When God called Jonah, he fled.

But that is not the way of a woman. Where in the Bible do you find a woman responding to God's call with equivocations, rationalizations, or alibis?

Mary said, "Behold, the handmaid of the Lord; be it unto me according to thy word." In other words, "I am Thine, O Lord, I have heard Thy voice" or "Take my life, and let it be consecrated, Lord, to Thee." (Both of these hymns were written by women.)

Why did Mary respond in this way? Because she was a woman. And because of the kind of woman she was.

Service, sacrifice, and submission are natural to women. We serve even when our hearts are troubled. We sacrifice even when we do not fully understand. We submit sometimes because we have not the strength to withstand but more often because through submission comes fulfillment.

Now there are two things I want to say about Mary before we close. Next week we shall continue Mary's story.

The first concerns the angel who visited her.

Some of you—perhaps most of you—do not believe in angels.

You say, "No angel ever spoke to me."

You say, "I never saw an angel or touched his hand."

You say, "Only children believe in angels."

You say, "Angels are a part of the fanciful poetry of religion, and we are not supposed to believe in them literally."

Very well. I shall not quarrel with you.

All I can say is that if you are right, then I'm a gullible old fool. For I believe in angels.

I can't say I've ever seen an angel, although I've a pretty good idea what one would look like. Ah, me! he'd be out of this world!

But angels have nudged my arm when I've stood at the kitchen sink. Angels have pointed the way when I have been lost in an endless labyrinth. Angels have placed my head on their shoulders when I have been despondent and blue. Angels have cheered me when I have nursed a broken heart. Angels have wiped my eyes when the death of a loved one has made me want to die.

God's messages and messengers are all about us.

But you have got to have eyes that see and you've got to have ears that hear. Eyes for the invisible and ears for the inaudible.

Some people never perceive anything.

They walk on the grass and never see a blade.

They enter a garden and never see a blossom.

They gaze at the mountains and never see their clearly cut outline against the sky.

They look into the faces of little children and never think of the Creator or of how life will fare for them or what will become of their souls.

The accents of God are various. His presence assumes many disguises.

The Book of Hebrews tells us that "some have entertained angels unawares."

I am sure that God adopts many masquerades. His angel comes to you in the form of a wee babe to whom you will give your energy and your heart. His angel comes to you as the voice of conscience or duty or loyalty. His angel comes asking you to undertake some responsibility, which will not be done if you do not do it. His angel comes in an idea or attitude that is strange to your natural disposition. His angel comes urging you to do this or that as a service to God's Kingdom. His angel comes through a conscience that refuses to be covered over with fudge frosting.

An angel appeared to Mary in one fashion. Angels appear to us according to who and what and where we are.

The second thing I want to say regarding Mary concerns the Virgin Birth.

I believe in the Virgin Birth because it is clearly a Biblical teaching and because it is clearly a teaching of the Church. Now the Bible was surely not written by dupes nor the church doctrine formulated by fools. Besides, twenty centuries of believers have tested and tried, believed and experienced, the matters contained in the Creed. Somewhere along the way someone would have conclusively proved an error if there were an error.

I know how wise and advanced we who live in the twentieth century are. Look at the tools and weapons we have devised to exterminate the human race! Yet I do not think all wisdom and all knowledge resides in us, and that all of our ancestors were intellectual and spiritual fuddy-duddies.

So I don't want to throw the baby out with the bath water, and I gladly accept as my rightful legacy any light and truth my fathers may wish to offer me.

Now before you say that the manner of Mary's conception is inconceivable just let me remind you of what we do believe.

We believe that a great fish swallowed Jonah and vomited him, hale and hearty, after three days.

We believe that a pit of ravenous lions did not devour Daniel.

We believe that three Hebrew children walked placidly and unsinged in a fiery furnace that was so hot that it burned to death the men who threw them in.

We believe that a voice spoke from a burning bush.

We believe that Moses rolled back the waters and walked on dry land.

We believe that Elijah was whisked to Glory in a fiery chariot.

We believe that Balaam's mule spoke with more understanding than his master.

We believe that the sun and the moon stood still in the Valley of Ajalon.

We believe that when seven priests, after walking around in circles for seven days, blew on rams' horns, the massive walls of Jericho fell down.

We believe that Samson singlehanded slew one thousand men with the jawbone of an ass.

We believe that Lot's wife was turned to salt.

We believe that God created the heavens and the earth and one day will create a new heaven and a new earth.

We believe all this and much more. My heavens! there's no end to what we believe. Yet some stumbling believers hesitate when they are confronted by the story of the Annunciation. As though a God were to be limited only when He seeks to reveal Himself as lover, redeemer, and savior.

But Mary, who above all should have been disbelieving, said, "Be it unto me according to thy word." In the classroom of the Lord she had learned that "with God nothing shall be impossible."

And that is a lesson we need to learn. "The world is charged with the grandeur of God," the poet says. And so it is. Miracles are scattered everywhere, like the colored leaves of autumn.

If you don't know what to make of this greatest of all miracles, patiently see what its meaning can make of you.

Meanwhile you will leave this class and enter for seven days into the commonplace world of sun, moon, and stars, of day and night, of fresh air and running water, of growth and character and loving sacrifice—no mean miracles these! —and next Lord's Day we shall continue to probe the unimaginable miracle that in a world like ours should be found an individual as gracious and as good as Mary of Nazareth.

And now we shall pause long enough to place our treasures in Heaven, "where neither moth nor rust doth corrupt, and where thieves do not break through nor steal." Amen and amen.

Virginia Discusses the Consequences of Doubt and Faith

Dear Sister Deborahites.

Last Lord's Day our topic was Mary, the mother of our Lord and the woman in the whole Bible to whom many of us—myself at any rate—respond with greatest sensitivity and love.

Sure enough, Monday morning's mail brought me a letter which was critical of my including Mary in our unpretentious little studies of some of the women of the Bible.

Had I said something disrespectful about Mary? Had I besmirched her spotless character? No, none of these things. What was wrong was that I had even mentioned her name.

"We Protestants don't believe in Mary," the letter explained.

I noticed that the envelope was postmarked "3 p.m." on Sunday. I presume the good Sister retired promptly from Sunday School, deprived herself of the Rector's splendid sermon on peace and of chicken dinner, or whatever she usually partakes of for Sunday dinner. One thing only claimed her time, thought, and emotions. She just must straighten up the leaning tower of Protestantism.

She added as a postscript that I would see her no more. She intended to seek out some sanctuary where God's Word was undefiled by the words of a woman.

After my roomers had snuffed out their lights and turned off their radios for the night, I reread the lesson which had apparently touched an open nerve.

I found that my only sin was that I had been so bold as to mention Mary by name.

Then I got to rummaging through my memories. I was not long in recollecting those thunderous days when the pulpit pounders and the foot stompers narrowed their sights to two mortal enemies of the Lord. They were the Pope and the devil—in that order.

The good Sister, who walks, it seems to me, in darkness and now seeks to coddle her prejudices at other shrines, is stirring up the cold coals in which were forged the weapons for the religious wars of other days.

In my extreme naïveté I had believed those days had long since passed and that the sour grapes our fathers ate no longer set their children's teeth on edge.

Old prejudices die hard, and even when we're sure they are dead, the slightest breeze stirs new life in them.

It is important that early in life you choose companionable prejudices, for the fact is that they are likely to stay with you for a lifetime.

I hope you won't think of me as a heretic if I say that the loyalties my heart cherishes are like concentric circles. The largest circle encloses all of God's children everywhere. I am not concerned if they are big or little, rich or poor, kings or peasants. My spiritual spectacles do not show me their skin color. My hearing makes no distinction between mumbo-jumbo and eloquent syntax. That they are human beings, fashioned in the image of the Almighty, makes them my brothers and sisters. God loves them, and I try to do likewise.

The second circle encloses all Christians. We share a tie that binds our hearts in Christian love. By accident of birth or by commitment—or both—we are named by a particular Name, and we stand on the same promises. Every Christian is a next of kin to every other Christian.

The third circle, a wee less larger than the others, encloses those within the Episcopal Church, a church I love and cherish. But to love my own church with a particular and partial love does not mean that I love others less. Perhaps for this reason I love others more. I hope so.

In my one woman's campaign to clear up the debris that clutters the highway to Glory, I find myself thoroughly sympathetic with an old preacher I once knew. When I was a little girl, this roving evangelist—his name was Jerry—would stop occasionally to ask my mother if he might chew off the grass in front of the house with his dull mower.

The lawn mower was the only dull thing about this ardent brother. He would say, "Your lawn needs shaving." Mother would reply, "It was cut four days ago." He would say, "I'm off today for parts unknown, and I'd better cut when I can." Mother would reply, "Well, all right, if you say so."

And Jerry would take after that grass as though he were pursuing a demon.

Even when mowing, Jerry had slung at his side a tin handbasin that flipped and flopped with each step he took.

Jerry was born a Methodist, but when he took to preaching his credentials were examined. He had no credentials, and so he was told he would have to preach to other folks.

He asked for a little elbow room among the Baptists, and they allowed that if his faith were sure, he could follow his calling among the unenlightened.

And so he did. But he never became a dyed-in-the-wool

Baptist. He carried the little tin handbasin so that he might be in constant readiness to sprinkle the Methodist-minded. Those who were Baptist-inclined, he obligingly immersed in the turtle-infested waters of Childer's Pond.

When questioned as to this unusual procedure of salvation, Jerry defended his behavior by saying, "Anything to get 'em into the Kingdom!"

Now to continue last Sunday's lesson.

We turned from the many complicated theological teachings regarding Mary so that we might know her as a young woman whom God singled out for His holy purpose of human redemption and as a young woman who did not question God's will.

But the story of Mary, beautiful in detail and language, is a pie crust without shortening if we fail to include the parallel story of Mary's kinswoman, Elizabeth.

Mary considered Elizabeth to be of extraordinary importance to her personal welfare. Why should we think otherwise?

Even before Gabriel had been sent to Mary, he had already delivered a message to Elizabeth's husband, a priest named Zacharias.

The couple are described by St. Luke as "righteous before God, walking in all the commandments and ordinances of the Lord blameless." Additionally, they "both were now stricken in years," and "they had no child."

Undoubtedly, Elizabeth had often thought of Sarah of old who became a mother when most women are grandmothers or great-grandmothers. And she knew of Hannah whose empty heart had never been filled with a child's love. I am sure Elizabeth had often shared Hannah's "bitterness of soul" and had long since prayed Hannah's prayer: "O Lord of hosts, if thou wilt indeed look on the affliction of thine handmaid, and remember me, and not forget thine handmaid, but wilt give unto thine hand-maid a man child, then I will give him unto the Lord all the days of his life."

The Lord had responded to the need of Sarah and Hannah, but Elizabeth knew now that for her no such miracle would occur.

What did she do? She did not question God's judgment. She did what a million other childless women have done. She gave herself to helping other women who had more children than they could manage. She loved the children of other women as though they were her own. Perhaps she thought wistfully of young Mary and how one day she would come to her when her womb was heavy.

Well, one day when old Zacharias was taking his turn at incense time in the temple, Gabriel appeared before him and told him that not only would Elizabeth bear a son but also that "many shall rejoice at his birth" for "he shall be great in the sight of the Lord" and "make ready a people prepared for the Lord."

What was the old priest's reply? The King James Version makes the reply seem appropriate: "Whereby shall I know this? for I am an old man, and my wife well stricken in years."

What he actually said was "Sorry, but I don't believe what you are saying" or "I don't think God sent you to me."

These might not be exactly Zacharias' words but they represent exactly Zacharias' tune.

All of which made Gabriel feel mighty indignant, and as a consequence of Zacharias' disbelief he was deprived of speech for nine long months.

It seems ironical to me that here was Zacharias at the altar where he repeated the holy words and affirmations of his fathers, prayed for the consolation of Israel, and

helped people to believe in God's presence and concern. Yet when God's messenger appeared at this holiest of holy places, Zacharias did not believe.

But that's true for most of us. We pray fervently and continuously, and then if our prayer is answered, we think it is too good to be true, and we start looking the gift horse in the mouth.

Elizabeth, on the other hand, rejoiced that "thus hath the Lord dealt with me in the days wherein he looked on me."

She seems not even to have been surprised—only delighted.

I sometimes think that women have a greater capacity to believe than men. I can't stand women preachers, but I wonder if something wonderful might happen if the women were to take over the church.

You remember that Joseph was in quite a quandary before the angel told him about Mary. He didn't know what to do, and it took him some time to realize that God had given him a responsibility.

Some people will tell you that there is a difference between men and women. Men are rational and women are emotional. I've never seen anything which would make me believe this. Quite the otherwise. I think the difference lies in the fact that women have a greater capacity to believe. (Our good Rector excepted, of course.) Perhaps it is that women are themselves creators of miracles. After having given birth to a child, nothing else seems beyond belief.

After the Annunciation, Mary, having no one else to tell such an overwhelming circumstance, went to the one most likely to understand, which would be Elizabeth herself. The trip from Nazareth to Ain Karim, where Elizabeth lived, was about one and an half hours by camel.

The salutation of Elizabeth and Mary's response comprise the outstanding classic of the entire Bible. I never read the Magnificat without a tingling to the very end of my fingers.

I think it was right and proper for Mary to go to Elizabeth. The young girl sought the wisdom and experience of the older woman.

Every young person needs older advisers. It is necessary that we fully respect the experience of these advisers, and with open minds weigh and consider the advice they offer. Don't forget that they have traveled the road before us. No matter how favorable our own circumstances seem, how wide the road, how bright the day, how good our tires, or how well we think we can drive, we can't know a road until we travel it. Hearing about it is not enough. We are obliged to travel over it.

Our advisers know just how fast we can take the curves and where the stop signs are. They can point out the ditches that the wise guys have been pulled out of. They are willing to ride beside us, and if we are wise, when we come to the danger zones, we will let them have the wheel. And while they slow down for the bumps, pass those who lag, and dodge the aggressors, we can, if we are smart, learn many things that even the gentlemen who print the road maps never dream of.

Youth is always the loser when it fails to recognize and absorb the wisdom that plain, ordinary living begets in those who have lived longer. Knowledge is what other people print on paper. Wisdom is what living writes, little by little and day by day, in our hearts.

Mary stayed with Elizabeth for three months or until John was born and Zacharias got back his tongue.

What Mary and Elizabeth talked about, heaven only knows. The Bible is silent at those points where we most want to hear and loudest sometimes at those points where we couldn't care less.

Maybe we don't really need a libretto for the song that filled that house back in the hill country. I think as women we know what they said day after day, while the mute Zacharias sat in the corner nursing his faithlessness.

Elizabeth passed along to Mary the favorite family recipes, household hints for this and that, and ways to find time and make time for all that a woman must accomplish in her own home.

Elizabeth told and retold the story of the agelong messianic anticipations of the Hebrew people. She helped Mary to understand her responsibilities and the aches and pains which her life would know.

Elizabeth helped Mary to prepare her mind and spirit for the Nativity, for the years of growth, for the moment of decision, for the months of teaching and their conflicts and misunderstandings, and for those hours when her beloved Son's precious body would be stretched upon a cross.

"It is all written in the books of our fathers," Elizabeth said.

"I know," replied Mary quietly.

"He will be despised and rejected by men."

"I know."

"A sword will pierce your heart."

"I know."

"He will turn from you and shape His decisions according to God's wishes, not yours."

"Yes, I know."

"But, Mary dear, God will fill your loneliness with a great love, and He will uphold you with His everlasting arms."

"Oh, I know that, too, Elizabeth. I know that, and I shall never forget."

116

And the branches of a tree in the dooryard seemed to sketch the shadow of a cross on the ground. As the rays of the afternoon sun lingered momentarily, Mary's eyes followed the shadow which seemed to stretch from time to infinity. "Be it unto me according to Thy word," Mary said softly.

After the baby John had been taken into the temple on the eighth day, Mary returned to Nazareth, where she must face the just man who loved her and would think she had been unfaithful to him. She would be a mockery before her people. They would not—could not—understand.

The warm hand of Elizabeth no longer rested upon her head. She needed the help of another human being. She needed Joseph as she had never thought it possible to need anyone.

She could do nothing other than to tell him the truth and then to abide by whatever decision of acceptance or disposal he made.

A quotation from an ancient Hebrew parchment was given to me long ago by a rabbi in Chicago. I do not know where he got it. I never thought to ask him. The words are these:

> And when the cousin of Elizabeth was come again to her native city, and into the house where she was born, Joseph sought her out, and when he beheld her, he wept. And Mary said unto him, "Hear ye me. Behold in me the handmaid of the Lord. Accept in me the sacrifice of Israel for the promised covenant with God, and in His name, turn thou not from me."
>
> Joseph, believing that which he did not understand, knelt before her and kissed her feet. And in the maid of the House of David there was majestic and wondrous beauty. Those who perceiving, looking upon her, felt as if they had seen God.

After nearly fifty years of respectable living, Joseph had espoused himself to marry a girl who was soon to bear a child. Concerning her predicament, she had told him the most unlikely story any man would ever hear.

Joseph felt trapped. The people who really knew him would say she was unfit for the ceremony he had committed himself to. Those who did not really know him would tell ribald stories about him behind his back. In either case, in their eyes he would be a fool.

Joseph did not know what to do.

But God knew.

He always does.

If we put ourselves in His keeping and then listen, He always tells us.

God sent an angel to Joseph to confirm this strangest of stories. And Joseph "took unto him his wife," which means that he took her from her home to his.

God had given Mary into the keeping of one who would protect both her and the Child who within a few months would lie at her breast.

Next Lord's Day we shall continue and conclude the story of this majestic woman whom God chose to be the mother of our Lord.

Before we take up the collection which, by God's grace, will be used to tell of Christ to the nations, let us all unite in prayer. And remember to close your eyes when praying.

Virginia
Relates
the Vagaries
of Motherhood

Good morning, dear Sisters.

I now feel that I am one of you. The feeling is good.

Please do not think of me as a one-woman invasion from another Sunday School class or as a missionary sent to you by the weary and worn women who, now past fifty, hope that I may guide you safely past the pitfalls into which they stumbled.

To tell you the truth, I am much more at home with persons of your age. Women of my own age bore me. They have so little left to look forward to that they spend too much of their time rehearsing things which happened to them before or after the Flood.

I think the warmth I find myself expressing for you comes from the fact that so many of you have taken time to call my number just to say hello or to show spontaneous friendliness. It warms the cockles of an old woman's heart to hear a voice say, "Morning, Virginia. Just called to say hello."

I still consider myself to be your "pro tem" teacher, but I feel less "pro tem" each Sunday.

Even the Rector seems to think we belong together now. He commends our increased attendance and the way we're helping to balance his budget with our class offerings.

Last Sunday after church I told him that we regularly closed our session by beseeching the Lord to put the right words into his mouth at sermontime. Knowing that he preaches from a carefully typed manuscript that he keeps on the back burner for nearly half a week, I added, "Of course, Rector, we are aware that you prepare your sermons and do not preach impromtulike, depending on the guidance of the Holy Ghost, but we pray that God may give you the right tone for the right words."

He seemed to be moved by our concern.

Brother Gregory stops me every Sunday now to check his gold watch with my wristwatch. I don't know why. He's been a railroad man for more than thirty years, and I'd be willing to wager a cookie to a doughnut that his watch *always* tells the precise time.

I think it must be his way of reminding me that this is a world of clocks and calendars—and that my class should close in thirty minutes.

I am reminded of one of our D.A.R. meetings in Washington. The usual state of confusion reigned in the halls of Constitution Hall.

My attention was drawn to a page, who had been appointed from a small Southern state and was trying to display a large and genuine willingness to assist anyone who might require assistance.

Her curls were disarranged, and her feet had entered that stage of torture described by the words, "My feet are killing me." But she kept her post, as though the state of the union depended upon her faithful discharge of duty.

One daughter from a big state in the practical North, supported by her trusty cane and bedecked with orchids, approached the page, and with the poise becoming a gentle woman, explained her dilemma. She had to catch a train, and she must know the correct time.

That's no problem, thought the page. She retired momentarily into a nearby room, peered closely at the severe face of an upright timepiece, and returned, gleefully reporting said time of day.

The good daughter at first registered signs of hysteria and then of collapse.

"It can't be!" she exclaimed.

"Oh, yes, but it can," insisted the page, who then led the bewildered daughter into the nearby room and pointed to the huge dial, thereby proving, I presume, that people from the South know the time of day.

The face of the anxious daughter relaxed, and she burst into a hip-hip hurrah laughter. "My dear," she explained to the astonished page, "this room is the museum, and that clock has not run for one hundred years!"

Now that you have patiently endured Virginia's little joke, we turn to the lesson.

Last Lord's Day we left Mary, the mother of our Lord, awaiting the hour of her motherhood.

You know too well the story of the star and the Wise Men, of the angelic choir and the shepherds, and of the flight of Joseph and Mary into Egypt. So I won't retell it now.

After the refugees returned to Nazareth, Jesus began that process which my mother called "outgrowing the crib." St. Luke writes with endearing simplicity that "Jesus increased in wisdom and stature, and in favour with God and man."

When Jesus was twelve His mother and Joseph took Him to the great temple in Jerusalem. Jesus had reached maturity, according to Jewish reckoning, and it was right and proper that He should become acquainted with God's House.

When on the homeward journey Mary and Joseph did

not find their Lad with the boys of His age, they returned to the temple, where Jesus was engaged in a conversation with the experts and interpreters of the Mosaic Law.

Mary asked Jesus why He had caused them so much fright by remaining behind, and Jesus said that already He knew that He belonged in God's House. Mary experienced what, sooner or later, every mother experiences: the moment when she is no longer as essential to her child as she has previously been.

This is a moment toward which every mother looks with a combined dread and expectancy. We don't want to admit that the fledgling must one day make his first solo flight. When the time comes, we say, "It is too soon. His wings are not strong enough." But the child leaves the perch, and when he returns he is never our child in the same way.

Mary remembered so many things. Above all was God's claim on her Son. Regretfully, wistfully, anxiously, she admitted that no longer could she expect Jesus to belong only to her.

The span of time between Jesus' twelfth and thirtieth years are stupidly called "the missing years." Almost we think of this as a dormant period or of marking time. Nothing could be further from the truth!

It is beyond all reasonable surmise that the Personality which rocked the world should have spent eighteen years thumping and bumping around in a carpenter's shop.

For one thing, I know that eyes other than His mother's watched His every move. Eyes had been focused on Him since that night long before when that star had lighted the sky above that stable. As He grew older, surveillance continued because of their great uneasiness regarding Him. At no time did the inheritors of Herod's fears not know where He was and what He was doing.

During those "missing years" Jesus was where He belonged, among His own people, in and out of the Nazareth home, in and out of the local synagogue, in and among groups of pious religionists. He was storing His mind with the promises of old. He was strengthening His spirit through meditation and prayer. Always He continued to be employed in His "Father's business." The enlightenment already within Him unfolded as it became increasingly clear what His Father's will required.

At no time were John and Jesus strangers. At no time did Elizabeth express regret that her son's role would be that of a forerunner or trailblazer for the greater work of Mary's Son. She had known and rejoiced in this from the beginning, and this knowledge she imparted to John.

Then in "the fulness of time" and surely with the understanding of Mary and Elizabeth—if, indeed, Elizabeth were permitted to live to this hour of decision—John moved from the hill country, began preaching repentance, and watched for the time when Jesus should step forward. "One mightier than I cometh" was John's constant message.

Jesus was baptized by John in the waters of the Jordan.

I do not know whether or not Mary was present.

I do know that her heart and her prayers were with Him.

Mary was directly responsible for Jesus' first miracle. At a wedding feast at Cana, near Nazareth, Mary called Jesus' attention to the host's embarrassment when the wine was depleted.

Jesus' reply to His mother seems abrupt in the Authorized Version, which reads, "Woman, what have I to do with thee?" Jesus' reply was simply an expression of His hesitation at that time and place to demonstrate the divine power resident in Him.

Mary understood her Son's hesitation, but she also knew

124

the power at His command. So she told the servants to do whatever Jesus might ask.

Having now witnessed the first of Jesus' mighty signs, Mary retired to Nazareth, where quietly and unobtrusively she followed His work, refusing to interfere until more than thirty months later when at Golgotha she came to console and comfort as only a mother can.

Every mother knows that the time must come when a child no longer needs her to instruct and guide. It should be a joyous time, but how hard it is to let our child move ahead on his own!

One of the guests at Cana was a very young man named John into whose keeping Jesus was to commit the care of His mother at the hour of His greatest physical agony and in whose home in Jerusalem she died at an age of perhaps sixty years.

Joseph had probably died when Jesus was twenty or twenty-one. For me there is much pathos in Joseph's life, and for me it seems disappointing—and almost unfair—that he could not live to witness the ministry of the Child for whom he had defied convention and risked the disdain and scorn of every friend he may have had.

I want for a minute or two to do some interpolating. That was the favorite word of a preacher I knew when I was a child. He was forever adding fancy embroidery to the edges of Bible stories. (I guess he must have bequeathed his needles to me. Hence my interpolating.)

What and who brought Mary to Jerusalem on Good Friday? I am sure it was John or someone who did his bidding. When Jesus was arrested in Gethsemane, He was certainly not deserted by John. In great grief he sought out Mary, wherever she may then have been, because John knew that she was the one person who could be depended upon to hold back the floodtide of catastrophe.

But John did not know, as she did, that Jesus was destined to die.

All of you know that, following the evasive hypocrisy of Pilate, Jesus was nailed to timbers of dogwood forming a Latin cross.

At the foot of the Cross stood three persons. They signify the trinity of Christianity—love, forgiveness, and service.

His mother represents that quality of love which all true mothers have personified since time began. When circumstances lash you and life crucifies you, your mother always is at hand to support and cherish you. No condition ever changes or lessens her love.

Next to Mary stood the harlot of Magdala. This should demonstrate for all time that the forgiveness of God can render even the most vile of us fit to stand beside our Lord.

Next to the women stood John. He represents faithful service and is indicative of all young men and women who commit their lives to pure and holy purposes.

The mighty few and somewhat scattered references to Mary in the Gospels seem to have been included primarily to clarify and establish the Virgin Birth of Jesus. Yet the Gospels stress that she did all that she was able. After Jesus' death and resurrection, she took His place among His disciples, and she was present at their baptism of fire.

The story of Mary of Nazareth is a compelling story of soul-piercing sorrow which, although sympathetically acknowledged by devout men, can truly be comprehended only by women who have experienced the co-creative bond with God and who by the divine benediction of birth have become mothers themselves.

For me the most expressively beautiful of all statuary is "Pietà" by Michelangelo. It shows, as you know, the seated figure of Mary holding in her arms and across her knees the lifeless body of Christ. The cold marble is vibrant with the warmth of maternal emotion and piteous grace. It depicts the only entirely pure, holy, unselfish, and God-given love on earth, the love of a mother for her child.

Dear Sisters, most of you are still young enough to have living mothers. If this is still your privilege, tell her before another sun sets that you love her and that you are eternally grateful for her guidance.

There are few things which I say to you that are worth remembering, and even these you will soon forget. But if you forget all else, I shall be satisfied if you promise not to wait until your mother's ears are deafened by death to speak those precious words. Later, of course, you will say them to someone else who may not even wish to listen.

If you open your hearts to your mothers, I know you will come to a better understanding of Mary's love for her Son, our Lord.

Well, dears, this brings to a close my interpretation of Mary. Her story has been told more eloquently and more beautifully by others. The greatest artists and poets have paid their tribute to her mother's love. When we look upon these canvasses or read these books, we always look beyond her to her Son.

My time is too quickly gone.

Before the collection is taken, please close your eyes for prayer.